PROPERTY AND CASUALTY INSU

Iowa License Exam Manual

Randall M. Costello, CMA, CPA

IOWA INSURANCE SEMINAR
PO BOX 922
CEDAR FALLS, IA 50613

E-mail: IowaInsuranceSeminar@gmail.com

Website: www.IowaInsuranceSeminar.com

ISBN-10: 1479160717
ISBN-13: 978-1479160716

Printed in the United States of America

TABLE OF CONTENTS

INTRODUCTION

It is important to note that the terms "property" and "casualty" include both the personal lines and commercial lines insurance market.

"Property insurance" includes both **personal property** and **commercial property**.
"Casualty insurance" includes both **personal casualty** and **commercial casualty**.

On the other hand, the terms "personal lines" and "commercial lines" refer to the market rather than the type of coverage.

"Personal lines" insurance refers to the **individual and family market** for property and casualty insurance.
"Commercial lines" insurance refers to the **business market** for property and casualty insurance.

Iowa licensing exams are available for both Property insurance and Casualty insurance.
Iowa licensing exams are also available for both Personal lines authority and Commercial lines subject matter.

This study manual is designed to prepare you for the Property and Casualty Insurance License Exams so you can sell property and casualty insurance to both individuals and businesses. Separate study manuals are available for the Personal lines and Commercial lines exams.

Note: A producer who holds a Personal lines authority can obtain Property and Casualty lines of authority upon successful completion of the Commercial insurance subject examination.

This manual is designed for a person to get licensed in Property and Casualty lines of authority by passing both the Property exam and the Casualty exam.

In this study manual, we are going to focus on the testing points necessary to pass the Property and Casualty Insurance license exams. The written text is based on the published exam outline containing the testing topics.

The Iowa laws, rules, and regulations, Insurance terms and related concepts, and Policy provisions and contract law material **is on both** the Property exam and the Casualty exam. These topics are found at the beginning of the manual on pages 2-22.

In the pages that follow, the insurance text and testing points will be on the left hand side. Sample questions are on the right hand side with the answer key at the bottom of the page.

Try to learn the material in small bites. Go paragraph by paragraph and question by question.

Note: This study manual does NOT contain actual exam questions. Actual exam questions are copyrighted intellectual property of the testing companies. It is illegal and unethical to disclose actual exam questions. However, this study manual does provide information and sample questions sufficient to pass the licensing test.

PROPERTY AND CASUALTY – IOWA SPECIFIC CONTENT

I. IOWA LAWS, RULES, AND REGULATIONS COMMON TO ALL LINES

A. Insurance Commissioner/Division

1. Broad powers and duties
The governor shall appoint subject to confirmation by the senate, a commissioner of insurance, who shall serve for four years.

The commissioner shall have power to examine and investigate into the affairs of every person engaged in the business of insurance in this state in order to determine whether such person has been or is engaged in any unfair method of competition or in any unfair or deceptive act or practice.

2. Examination of records
The commissioner examines the activities, operations, financial condition, and affairs of all persons transacting the business of insurance in this state.

The state commissioner can inspect the business records of a company or agency at any time for any valid reason because of the powers defined by state laws. Domestic companies must be examined at least once every 5 years.

The Commissioner may accept an examination report on any foreign or alien insurer licensed in Iowa as prepared by the regulatory authority in the company's state of domicile.

3. Hearings The commissioner may give notice of a hearing to any such person engaging in any unfair method of competition or any unfair or deceptive act or practice. The hearing shall not be less than 10 days after notice of a hearing is served.

4. Penalties shall not exceed $1,000 for each violation, not to exceed $10,000. If the agent should have known the act was a violation, not more than $5,000 for each violation, not to exceed $50,000 in any 6 month period.

The commissioner may place on probation, suspend, revoke, or refuse to issue or renew a producer's license or may levy a civil penalty for writing bad checks/credit cards to the division or testing service, failing to report any administrative action or criminal prosecution taken against the producer or failure to report the termination of a resident license, or acting as an insurance producer through persons not licensed as insurance producers or taking any action to circumvent the spirit of these rules and the Iowa insurance statues.

5. A cease and desist order will be issued if the commissioner finds that a producer has engaged in an unfair trade practice. Monetary penalties, suspension, or revocation of license may also be ordered.

B. Licensing Requirements

1. Applications
An applicant applying for an examination shall remit a nonrefundable fee to an outside testing service and pass a written exam. An individual who fails to appear for the examination as scheduled or fails to pass the examination shall reapply for an examination and remit all required fees and forms before being rescheduled for another examination.

A person **applying for a resident insurance producer license** shall make application to the commissioner on the uniform application.

The individual must:
- Be at least 18 years old.
- Not have committed any act that is a ground for denial, suspension, or revocation.
- Pay a license fee of $50.
- Pass the exam.
- Have the requisite character and competence.

Assumed names
An insurance producer doing business under any name other than the insurance producer's legal name is required to notify the commissioner prior to using the assumed name.

3

1. The insurance commissioner is

A. Elected every 4 years
B. Elected every 6 years
C. Appointed by the governor and confirmed by the senate
D. Appointed by the governor and confirmed by the house

2. The term of office for the Iowa insurance commissioner is for a period of

A. 2 years
B. 3 years
C. 4 years
D. 6 years

3. The power to examine and investigate into the affairs of every person engaged in the business of insurance resides with the

A. Attorney General
B. Governor
C. Commissioner of Insurance
D. House Judiciary Committee

4. Domestic companies must be examined by the commissioner at least once every

A. Year
B. 2 years
C. 3 years
D. 5 years

5. The commissioner may give notice of a hearing to any such person engaging in any unfair method of competition or any unfair or deceptive act or practice. The hearing shall not be less than how many days after notice of a hearing is served?

A. 10 days
B. 15 days
C. 20 days
D. 30 days

6. If a person knew or reasonably should have known the person was in violation of insurance trade practices, the penalty shall not exceed

A. $1,000 for each violation, maximum of $10,000
B. $3,000 for each violation, maximum of $30,000
C. $5,000 for each violation, maximum of $50,000
D. $10,000 for each violation, maximum of $100,000

7. If the commissioner finds that a producer has engaged in an unfair trade practice, commissioner may NOT

A. Impose a monetary penalty
B. Impose a prison sentence
C. Suspend the producer's license
D. Revoke the producer's license

8. What will be issued if the commissioner finds that a producer has engaged in an unfair trade practice?

A. A writ of habeas corpus
B. A court subpoena
C. A cease and desist order
D. A writ of prohibition

9. A person applying for a resident insurance producer license would NOT be required to

A. Be at least 18 years of age
B. Be of good repute
C. Successfully complete an exam
D. Serve a two year internship

10. An insurance producer doing business under any name other than the insurance producer's legal name is required to

A. Cease and desist from using the assumed name
B. Use the assumed name only in conversations
C. Sign the application using both the producer's legal name and assumed name
D. Notify the commissioner prior to using the assumed name

1-C   2-C   3-C   4-D   5-A   6-C   7-B   8-C   9-D   10-D

4

2. Change of address

A licensee shall inform the commissioner of a change of address within 30 days of the change.

Failure to timely inform the commissioner of a change in legal name or address may result in a late fee of $100.

3. Licensing examinations

Applications and fees for examinations are conducted by the outside testing service

www.pearsonVUE.com

Examination results are valid for 90 days after the date of the test.

Failure to apply for licensure within 90 days after the examination is passed shall void the examination results.

4. Resident licensing

To receive an amended license for an additional line of authority:

- Submit a completed uniform application form.
- Pass an examination for each line of authority requested.
- Pay the fee to amend an insurance producer license.

A producer who holds a personal lines authority (authority number 16) can obtain property and casualty lines of authority (authority numbers 21 and 22) upon successful completion of the commercial insurance subject examination.

Issuance of license

An insurance producer license is for a term of **3 years.**

Nonresident licensing

A nonresident person shall receive a nonresident insurance license if the person

- Is currently licensed as an insurance producer and is in good standing in the person's home state.
- Has submitted the proper request for licensure and has paid the required fees.
- Has submitted to the commissioner the application for licensure that the person submitted to the person's home state or a completed uniform application.
- Person's home state awards nonresident insurance licenses to residents of this state on the same basis.

A nonresident insurance producer who moves from one state to another state or a resident insurance producer who moves from this state to another state shall file a change of address and provide certification from the new resident state within 30 days of the change of legal residence. No fee or license application is required.

5. Temporary license

Temporary licenses may be issued for 90 days, with extensions allowed, but in no event for longer than **180 days.**

It may be issued to the surviving spouse or court-appointed personal representative of a licensed insurance producer who dies or becomes mentally or physically disabled, or to allow adequate time for the sale of the insurance business owned by the insurance producer, or for the recovery or return of the insurance producer to the business, or for the training and licensing of new personnel to operate the insurance producer's business.

1. A licensee shall inform the commissioner by any means acceptable to the commissioner of a change of address within how many days of the change?

A. 15 days
B. 20 days
C. 30 days
D. 45 days

2. Failure to timely inform the commissioner of a change in legal name or address within 30 days may result in

A. A monetary penalty
B. Suspension of license
C. Revocation of license
D. Censure of the producer

3. After the date of the test, examination results are valid for

A. 30 days
B. 60 days
C. 90 days
D. 120 days

4. Any licensed insurance producer wanting to add an amendment to the license to become licensed in an additional line of authority does NOT have to

A. Submit a completed uniform application form
B. Complete additional continuing education
C. Pay the fee to amend a producer license
D. Pass an examination for each line of authority requested to be added

5. An insurance producer license shall remain in effect for a term of

A. 1 year
B. 2 years
C. 3 years
D. 4 years

6. All of the following are necessary for a nonresident to receive a nonresident insurance license EXCEPT

A. The person is currently licensed as an insurance producer
B. The person has submitted the proper request for licensure
C. The person lives in a bordering state
D. The person's home state awards nonresident insurance producer licenses to residents of this state on the same basis.

7. Which of the following is NOT necessary for a nonresident to receive a nonresident license?

A. Paying the required fees
B. Good standing the person's home state
C. Reciprocity with the home state
D. Living in the Midwest Zone

8. A resident insurance producer who moves from this state to another state shall file a change of address and provide certification from the new resident state within

A. 30 days   C. 90 days
B. 60 days   D. 120 days

9. Temporary licenses will be issued for 90 days, with extensions allowed, but in no event for longer than

A. 180 days   C. 2 years
B. 1 year   D. Age 65

10. Unless the commissioner deems that the public interest will best be served, the commissioner would NOT issue a temporary insurance license to

A. The surviving spouse of a licensed producer
B. A producer who fails to get the proper CE credits
C. To a member of a business entity licensed as an insurance producer
D. The court-appointed personal representative of a licensed producer

1-C   2-A   3-C   4-B   5-C   6-C   7-D   8-A   9-A   10-B

6. Exemptions from examination

A license as an insurance producer shall not be required an insurer, of those not selling, soliciting or receiving a commission, executive, administrative, managerial, clerical employees only indirectly related to the sale, solicitation, or negotiation of insurance, or a licensed attorney providing surety bonds incident to the attorney's practice.

An examination shall not be required of a person to obtain an insurance producer license for any line of authority previously held in the prior state except where the commissioner determines otherwise by regulation.

7. Denial, renewal, termination of licenses

The commissioner may place on probation, suspend, revoke, or refuse to issue or renew an insurance producer's license or may levy a civil penalty for:

a. Providing incorrect, misleading, incomplete, or materially untrue information in the license application.
b. Violating any insurance laws, or violating any regulation, subpoena, or order of the commissioner or of a commissioner of another state.
c. Obtaining or attempting to obtain a license through misrepresentation or fraud.
d. Improperly withholding, misappropriating, or converting any moneys or properties received in the course of doing insurance business.
e. Intentionally misrepresenting the terms of an actual or proposed insurance contract or application for insurance.
f. Having been convicted of a felony.
g. Having admitted or been found to have committed any unfair insurance trade practice or fraud.
h. Using fraudulent, coercive, or dishonest practices, or demonstrating incompetence, untrustworthiness, or financial irresponsibility in the conduct of business in this state or elsewhere.
i. Having an insurance producer license, or its equivalent, denied, suspended, or revoked in any other state, province, district, or territory.
j. Forging another's name to an application for insurance or to any document related to an insurance transaction.
k. Improperly using notes or any other reference material to complete an examination for an insurance license.
l. Knowingly accepting insurance business from an individual who is not licensed.
m. Failing to comply with an administrative or court order imposing a **child support** obligation.
n. Failing to comply with an administrative or court order related to **repayment of loans to the college student aid commission.**
o. Failing to pay **state income tax** or comply with any administrative or court order directing payment of state income tax.
p. Failing or **refusing to cooperate** in an investigation by the commissioner.

License renewal

Failure to renew a license and pay appropriate fees prior to the expiration date of the license will result in expiration of the license.

An insurance producer who allows the license to lapse may have the license reinstated within 12 months from the due date by paying the renewal fee and the reinstatement fee, without the necessity of passing a written examination.

Reporting of actions

A producer shall report to the division any actions taken against the producer in another state.

Administrative action is to be reported within 30 days of the final disposition of the matter.

Criminal prosecution is to be reported within 30 days of the initial pretrial hearing date.

1. Which of the following would be required to take an insurance licensing examination?

A. A sales employee soliciting insurance
B. A person not receiving a commission
C. A licensed attorney providing surety bonds incident to the attorney's practice
D. An administrative employee only indirectly related to the sale of insurance

2. A licensing exam would NOT be required of

A. A clerical employee quoting prices to a prospective customer
B. An executive negotiating the sale of insurance
C. An insurer
D. A managerial employee receiving a commission

3. The commissioner may terminate a producer's license for

A. Changing the producer's address
B. Changing the producer's name
C. Having been convicted of a felony
D. Having multiple company appointments

4. The commissioner may NOT penalize an insurance producer for failing to pay

A. Child support   C. State income tax
B. College student loans   D. Estimated taxes

5. The commissioner would NOT penalize an insurance producer for

A. Improperly using notes on an insurance exam
B. Knowingly accepting insurance business from an individual who is licensed
C. Attempting to obtain a license through misrepresentation or fraud
D. Forging another's name to an application

6. If the commissioner denies an application for a license, the commissioner would NOT

A. Issue a cease and desist order
B. Notify the applicant of the denial of application
C. Advise the applicant in writing the reason for denial of application
D. Conduct a hearing at the request of the applicant

7. A producer's license may be revoked for

A. Failing to join a professional organization
B. Failing to get a company appointment
C. Failing to earn a commission
D. Failing to cooperate with the commissioner

8. Failure to renew a license and pay appropriate fees prior to the expiration date of the license will result in

A. A 30 day grace period
B. A 60 day grace period
C. Expiration of the license
D. A 90 grace period

9. A lapsed license may be reinstated after the due date by paying the renewal fee and reinstatement fee within

A. 1 month   C. 12 months
B. 6 months   D. 18 months

10. The reporting of administrative action or criminal prosecution taken against the producer in another state is to be reported to the Iowa Insurance Division within

A. 30 days   C. 60 days
B. 45 days   D. 90 days

1-A   2-C   3-C   4-D   5-B   6-A   7-D   8-C   9-C   10-A

8

8. Commissions and referral fees An insurance company shall not pay, and a person shall not accept, any commission, service fee, brokerage or other valuable consideration unless the person performing the service held a valid license for the line of insurance for which the service was rendered at the time the service was performed.

An insurer or a producer may pay a nominal fee for referrals if the same fee is paid for each referral whether or not the referral results in an insurance transaction.

9. Company appointments An individual insurance producer who acts as an agent of an insurer must be appointed by that insurer. An insurance producer who is not acting as an agent of an insurer need not be appointed. A business entity is not required to be appointed.

The insurer must file notice of appointment within 30 days from the date the contract is executed or the first insurance application is submitted.

Appointment termination of a producer must be filed within 30 days of the date the insurer terminated its agency relationship with the producer.

10. Continuing education
These rules do not apply to:
- A nonresident producer who resides in a state or district having a continuing education (CE) requirement for insurance producers.

- A resident producer who holds qualification 5 (surety) or 18 (credit life, accident and health insurance).

- Licensed attorneys who are also producers who submit proof of completion of continuing legal education for the appropriate calendar years during the CE term, pay the continuing education fee set and otherwise comply with the producer license renewal procedures.

- A producer who serves full–time in the armed forces of the United States of America on active duty during a substantial part of the CE term and who submits evidence of such service.

Definitions
CE term means the **three–year–one–month** period beginning the first day of the producer's birth month and ending on the last day of the producer's birth month in the renewal year.

Every licensed resident producer must complete a minimum of **36 credits** for each CE term in courses approved by the division. A producer **cannot carry over CE credits** from one CE term to the next.

Three (3) of these credits must be in the subject of ethics and up to **18 credits** may be **through self–study courses.**

A resident producer who holds qualification for only a crop insurance line of authority must complete all training and continuing education requirements imposed by the federal Risk Management Association (if any) and complete 18 credits of continuing education, 3 of which must be in the area of ethics.

A producer may not receive CE credit for courses taken prior to the issuance of an initial license.

A producer may elect to comply with the CE requirements by taking and passing the appropriate licensing examination for each qualification held by the producer.

Proof of completion of continuing education requirements
Producers are required to demonstrate compliance with the CE requirements at the time of license renewal.

Producers are required to maintain a record of all CE courses completed by keeping the original certificates of completion for 4 years after the end of the year of attendance.

9

1. Which of the following would be required to be appointed by an insurer?

A. An insurance broker who is not affiliated with the insurer
B. An insurance producer who is not acting as an agent of an insurer
C. An individual insurance producer who acts as an agent of an insurer
D. A business entity

2. The insurer must file notice of appointment within how many days from the date the contract is executed or the first insurance application is submitted?

A. 15 days
B. 30 days
C. 45 days
D. 60 days

3. The insurer must file notice of appointment termination of a producer within how many days from the date the insurer terminated its agency relationship with the producer?

A. 15 days
B. 30 days
C. 45 days
D. 60 days

4. The continuing education rules would apply to

A. A producer who serves full-time in the armed forces
B. A resident insurance producer who holds qualification in life insurance
C. A licensed attorney who is a producer and submits proof of continuing legal education
D. A resident insurance agent who holds only a qualification in surety insurance

5. A CE term is based on

A. Every 3 calendar years
B. Every calendar year
C. The producers first month of licensure
D. The producers birth month

6. Every licensed resident producer must complete a minimum of how many credits for each CE term?

A. 12 credits
B. 24 credits
C. 36 credits
D. 30 credits

7. The number of CE credits required in the subject of ethics for every licensed resident producer for each CE term is

A. 3 credits
B. 6 credits
C. 9 credits
D. 18 credits

8. Continuing education requirements do NOT allow

A. Compliance by passing the appropriate licensing examination for each qualification held by the producer.
B. Up to 18 CE credits for self-study
C. An instructor to receive credit for teaching a CE class
D. A producer to receive CE credit for courses taken prior to the issuance of an initial license

9. A producer may comply with the CE requirement in all of the following ways EXCEPT

A. Complete an examination for that subject line
B. Self-study courses
C. Publishing research articles
D. Classroom courses

10. Producers are required to maintain a record of all CE courses completed by keeping the original certificates of completion for how many years after the end of the year of attendance?

A. 1 year
B. 2 years
C. 3 years
D. 4 years

1-C   2-B   3-B   4-B   5-D   6-C   7-A   8-D   9-C   10-D

C. Unfair and Deceptive Practices

1. Discrimination Making or permitting unfair discrimination between persons with essentially the same hazards is forbidden. A contract shall not be denied to an individual based solely on the fact that such individual has been or is believed to have been a victim of domestic abuse.

2. Misrepresentation of the benefits, advantages, conditions, or terms of any insurance policy including false statements for the purpose of obtaining a fee from any agent or individual.

Twisting is any action for the purpose of inducing (convincing) an insured to drop a policy of one insurer in order to replace it with a policy of another insurer or encouraging prospective clients to lapse a policy to their detriment.

3. Rebating An offer by an agent to give a part of the agent's commission to a prospective insured is an illegal rebate.

4. Advertising in any way which is untrue, deceptive or misleading is an unfair trade practice.

5. Claims settlement Unreasonably delaying payment of claim, or misrepresenting policy provisions to claimant, or failure to give a reasonable explanation for denying a claim.

6. Defamation Making oral or written statements directly or indirectly which are derogatory or maliciously critical of another person or disparaging of other insurers.

7. Boycott, coercion and intimidation tending to result in unreasonable restraint of, or monopoly in, the business of insurance are unfair trade practices.

8. Iowa Insurance Fraud Act The insurance fraud bureau investigates fraudulent claims. Bureau investigators have the same powers as law enforcement officers. The purpose of the act is to reduce premiums and to assist prosecutors of criminal fraud.

A person who knowingly presents false statements in relation to an insurance policy is guilty of a class D felony. An insurer has 60 days to notify the fraud bureau of receipt of any claim it believes to be fraudulent.

D. Guaranty Association

The purpose of this Guaranty Association is to protect persons against failure in the performance of contractual obligations because of the impairment or insolvency of the member insurer which issued the policies or contracts.

To provide this protection, an association of insurers is created to enable the guaranty of payments of benefits up to $300,000 ($100 deductible) and of continuation of coverages. Members of the association are subject to assessment to provide funds to carry out the purpose.

"A person shall not advertise or publish, in connection with the sale of an insurance policy, that claims under the insurance policy are subject to this chapter or will be paid by the Iowa Insurance Guaranty Association."

1. Unfair discrimination would include

A. Charging the same rate for individuals of the same class
B. Discrimination on the basis of different hazards
C. Discrimination on the basis of domestic abuse
D. Charging the same rate for the same hazards

2. Making false or fraudulent statements relative to an application for an insurance policy for the purpose of obtaining a commission is

A. A misrepresentation   C. Rebating
B. A warranty   D. Coercion

3. Which of the following is NOT an illegal rebate?

A. Selling stock of any insurance company as an inducement to policyholders
B. Paying bonuses to policyholders out of company surplus in a fair and equitable manner
C. Giving anything of value whatsoever not specified in the contract as an inducement to the policyholder
D. Offering any inducement not specified in the contract

4. The definition of advertising would NOT include

A. TV scripts
B. Billboards
C. Communications not intended for dissemination to the public
D. Sales talks and presentations for use by producers

5. Committing a general business practice of not attempting in good faith to effectuate prompt, fair and equitable settlements of claims in which liability has become reasonably clear is known as

A. Negligence per se
B. An unfair claims settlement practice
C. Twisting
D. Stretching claims payable

6. Literature which is maliciously critical of or derogatory of any person and is calculated to injure such person is known as

A. Defamation
B. False advertising
C. Coercion
D. Intimidation

7. Unfair trade practices would NOT include

A. Boycott
B. Contractual agreement
C. Coercion
D. Intimidation

8. When a person knowingly makes false statements in relation to an insurance policy, the person is guilty of a

A. Solicitation error
B. Simple misdemeanor
C. Class D felony
D. Mea culpa

9. The purpose of the Iowa Insurance Guaranty Association is to

A. Enable the payments of benefits if an insurer becomes insolvent
B. Insure the policies of applicants
C. Enable the payment of benefits regardless of insurer solvency
D. Pay claims of an insolvent insurer without limit

10. The Iowa Insurance Guaranty Association is funded by

A. Sales tax revenue
B. Taxpayers
C. Premium taxes
D. Assessing member insurers

1-C   2-A   3-B   4-C   5-B   6-A   7-B   8-C   9-A   10-D

PROPERTY AND CASUALTY INSURANCE TERMS AND RELATED CONCEPTS

Insurance is a contract or device for transferring the risk of loss from a person, business or organization to an insurance company that agrees, in exchange for a premium, to pay for losses through an accumulation of premiums.

Law of Large Numbers states that the larger the number of insureds, the greater the probability that *actual* loss experience will equal expected loss experience. In some instances, insurers can virtually eliminate their risk of loss by securing a large enough number of insureds in an insured group.

Insurable interest occurs when a person stands to lose life or property. In property and casualty insurance an insurable interest must exist at the time of loss.

Risk is the uncertainty or chance of loss. Risk can be **speculative** (an opportunity for gain that may result in a loss) or **pure** (involves only the possibility of loss or no loss). There is no compensating chance of gain. It exists whether you want it to or not. Insurance deals with pure risk.

Risk management is a scientific approach to the problem of dealing with pure risks. An example of risk management is the elimination of a hazard.

Hazard A hazard is a condition that creates or increases the probability of a loss.

- **Physical** hazards are those that increase the possibility of a loss such as flammable substances.

- **Moral** hazard. dishonesty, lack of integrity.

- **Morale** hazard. careless attitude, indifference, failure to care

Peril The cause of possible loss; the event insured against, e.g., fire.

Loss is the unintentional decline in, or disappearance of, value due to a contingency.

- **Direct loss** Financial loss resulting directly from a loss to property.

- **Indirect loss** is the result or consequence of a direct loss. (consequential losses or loss of use)

Loss Valuation
Actual cash valuation The cost to replace an item of property at the time of loss, less an allowance for depreciation.

Replacement cost The cost to replace a damaged or destroyed item of property, without deduction for depreciation.

Market valuation is the highest estimated price that a buyer would pay and a seller would accept for an item in an open and competitive market.

Stated value insurance policies cover property for a previously agreed upon price regardless of the actual cash value. Sometimes called "Assigned Value Insurance"

Salvage value is the estimated selling value of any asset, after it has reached the end of service life or its value has depreciated substantially.

Loss settlement provisions including consent to settle a loss Claim settlement options include paying the value of the damaged property, replacing or repairing, taking the property at the agreed value or repair, rebuild or replace with other property of like kind and quality.

Right of salvage Damaged property that can be retrieved, reconditioned and sold to reduce an insured loss.

Abandonment A policy condition stating that the insured cannot abandon damaged property to the insurer and demand to be reimbursed for its full value.

1. Insurance is a contract for

A. Retaining risk
B. Avoiding risk
C. Controlling risk
D. Transferring risk

2. The law of large numbers states that the larger the number of insureds,

A. The fewer the actual number of losses
B. The less reliable the predictability of the number of losses
C. The more reliable the predictability of the expected losses
D. The lower the chance of the insurance company eliminating risk

3. An insurable interest in property insurance

A. Is not required
B. Encourages speculative wagering
C. Must be present at the time of loss
D. Must be present at the inception of the policy

4. Insurance deals with pure risk such as

A. Gambling
B. Damage to your auto
C. Starting a new business
D. Investing in the stock market

5. An example of a moral hazard would be

A. An arsonist
B. Icy sidewalks
C. Careless driving
D. An open gas can in the garage

6. An example of an indirect loss would be

A. Loss of jewelry due to theft
B. Loss of a car due to collision
C. Loss of a home due to tornado
D. Loss of rental income due to fire

7. Actual cash value is

A. A functional equivalent
B. Coverage up to the agreed amount
C. Replacement cost less depreciation
D. Based upon free market conditions

8. Loss settlement provisions do NOT include

A. Repairing the damaged property
B. Rebuilding the damaged property
C. Paying the value of the damaged property
D. Requiring the insured to sue the insurer to collect for damaged property

9. Which party has the right of salvage?

A. Insurer
B. Insured
C. Negligent third party
D. State insurance division

10. Loss settlement options do NOT include

A. Taking the property at the agreed value
B. Abandonment of damaged property to the insurer
C. Paying the value of the damaged property after consenting to settle a loss
D. Replacing the damaged property with other property of like kind and quality

1-D   2-C   3-C   4-B   5-A   6-D   7-C   8-D   9-A   10-B

Proximate cause An action that, in a natural and continuous sequence, produces a loss.

Deductible Dollar amount the insured must pay on each loss to which the deductible applies. The insurance company pays the remainder of each covered loss up to the policy limits.

Indemnity Principle of insurance that provides that when a loss occurs, the insured should be restored to the approximate financial condition occupied before the loss occurred, no better or no worse.

Limits of liability Maximum amount the insurance company will pay for a particular loss, or for losses sustained during a period of time. It is also called limit of coverage, limit of insurance and policy limit.

Coinsurance/insurance to value Policy condition that requires an insured to pay part of a loss if the amount of insurance carried on property is less than a specified percentage of the value of the property at the time of loss.

Occurrence A loss that occurs at a specific time and place or over a period of time.

Accident A loss that occurs at a specific time and place.

Cancellation Termination of an insurance policy by the insured or the insurance company during the policy period.

Nonrenewal Decision made by an insured or insurance company to not continue coverage for another policy period after the current policy period expires.

Vacancy The absence of both people and property from a premises.

Unoccupancy The absence of people from a premises.

A vacant building has a greater exposure to loss than an unoccupied building.

Liability Losses arising from the unintentional negligent damage to property of others or to their body.

Absolute liability is imposed without the need to prove fault or negligence, e.g., workers compensation, defective products.

Strict liability is also known as absolute liability.

Vicarious liability imposes responsibility upon one person for the failure of another, with whom the person has a special relationship (such as parent and child, employer and employee, or owner of vehicle and driver), to exercise such care as a reasonably prudent person would use under similar circumstances.

1. Bodily injury liability Includes injury, sickness, disease, and death resulting from any of these at any time.

2. Property damage liability Damage to or destruction of property of others, including loss of use of the property.

3. Personal injury liability Injury other than bodily injury arising out of such things as libel, slander, false arrest, wrongful entry, violation of privacy, and malicious prosecution.

Negligence The lack of reasonable care that is required to protect others from the unreasonable chance of harm.

Binder Oral or written statement that provides immediate insurance protection for a specified period. Designed to provide temporary coverage until a policy is issued or denied.

Endorsements Documents attached to an insurance policy that changes the policy's original terms, conditions and coverages in some way.

Limitations Policy language that eliminates or reduces coverage under certain circumstances or when specified conditions apply.

1. A negligent act or peril causing damage to another person or property is known as

A. Causational cause
B. A concurrent cause
C. The proximate cause
D. An intervening cause

2. Which principle of insurance restores the insured to the approximate financial condition occupied before the loss?

A. Indemnity
B. Stated value
C. Limit of liability
D. Insurance to value

3. A loss that occurs at a specific time and place or over a period of time is

A. A peril
B. An event
C. An accident
D. An occurrence

4. The absence of both people and property from the premises is

A. Vacancy
B. Desolation
C. Unoccupancy
D. Abandonment

5. The absence of people from the premises is

A. Vacancy
B. Desolation
C. Unoccupancy
D. Abandonment

6. Liability that is imposed without the need to prove fault or negligence is

A. Absolute liability
B. Vicarious liability
C. Negligent liability
D. Personal injury liability

7. Liability that is imputed from one to another is

A. Strict
B. Absolute
C. Vicarious
D. Compensatory

8. Personal injury liability does NOT include

A. Libel
B. Slander
C. False arrest
D. Bodily injury

9. A temporary contract proving insurance to be in force is called a

A. Binder
B. Voidable contract
C. Prima-facie contract
D. Contract of adhesion

10. A document attached to an insurance policy that modifies the terms or conditions of the contract is

A. A codicil
B. An addendum
C. An endorsement
D. A supplementary agreement

1-C   2-A   3-D   4-A   5-C   6-A   7-C   8-D   9-A   10-C

Medical Payments are provided for bodily injury claims.

Blanket vs. Specific
Blanket insurance coverage is a single amount of insurance that is provided to all locations.

Specific insurance coverage is a single amount of insurance for a specific location.

Theft, Burglary, Robbery, Mysterious Disappearance

Theft means any unlawful taking of property of others, including burglary and robbery.

Burglary is the taking of property by a person unlawfully entering or leaving the premises as evidenced by visible signs of forced entry or exit.

Robbery is the taking or attempted taking of property by one who has caused or threatened to cause bodily harm, or committed a witnessed, obviously unlawful act.

Mysterious disappearance Vanishing of property with no explanation.

Warranties Specific agreements between the insured and the insurer that becomes a part of the insurance policy. A breach of warranty can void the policy.

Representations Statements on an insurance application that the applicant believes are true. A representation is not considered a matter to which the parties contract, so a policy cannot be voided on the basis of a representation.

Concealment The withholding of a material fact involved in the contract on which the insurer relies.

The **Deposit Premium** is an estimated premium subject to a **Premium Audit** before calculating a final premium.

Certificate of insurance Written form that verifies a policy has been written. Provides a summary of the coverage provided under the policy.

Damages
Compensatory damages may be either
> **General damages** provide compensation for pain and suffering, disfigurement, loss of limbs, and other subjective losses.

> **Special damages** provide compensation for hospital expenses, doctor expenses and other objective losses.

Punitive damages are over and above general damages to punish the negligent party.

Compliance with provisions of Fair Credit Reporting Act Insurance companies wanting an investigative report on the credit and background history of an applicant for underwriting purposes must give notification to the insured within 3 days after the request for an investigative report. If coverage is declined, the applicant has a right to be informed of the name and address of the reporting agency.

PROPERTY AND CASUALTY POLICY PROVISIONS AND CONTRACT LAW

"DICED" is the acronym to help remember the 5 major sections of an insurance policy.

1. Declarations Section of an insurance contract that shows who is insured, what property or risk is covered, when and where the coverage is effective, and how much coverage applies.

2. Insuring agreement Section of an insurance policy that describes what is covered and the perils the policy insures against.

3. Conditions Portion of an insurance policy that describes the rights and duties of the insured and the insurance company under the policy.

4. Exclusions Section of an insurance policy that lists property, perils, persons, or situations that are not covered under the policy.

5. Definitions Section of an insurance policy that clarifies the meaning of certain terms used in the policy.

1. When a person wants to cover property at any location, they would most likely purchase

A. Blanket insurance
B. Specific insurance
C. Direct loss insurance
D. Agreed amount insurance

2. The taking of property from inside the premises by a person unlawfully entering or leaving the premises as evidenced by visible marks is

A. Theft
B. Robbery
C. Burglary
D. Mysterious disappearance

3. If someone takes or attempts to take property while threatening bodily harm, it is known as

A. Theft
B. Robbery
C. Burglary
D. Pilfering

4. A statement made on an insurance application that the applicant believes is true is a

A. A warranty
B. An opinion
C. A concealment
D. A representation

5. The intentional withholding of information of a material nature by an applicant is known as

A. Waiver
B. Estoppel
C. Ambiguity
D. Concealment

6. General damages include

A. Objective losses
B. Doctor expenses
C. Pain and suffering
D. Hospital expenses

7. Special damages include

A. Loss of limbs
B. Disfigurement
C. Subjective losses
D. Surgical expenses

8. The Fair Credit Reporting Act governs two consumer reports: the regular consumer report and the investigative consumer report. Written notice for a request for an investigative report must be sent not later than how many days after the report is ordered?

A. 3 days
B. 5 days
C. 10 days
D. 15 days

9. The Declarations section of an insurance contract would NOT include the

A. Named perils
B. Name of the insured
C. Location of the property
D. Effective date of coverage

10. Which of the following is NOT a major section of the insurance contract?

A. Conditions
B. Warranties
C. Exclusions
D. Declarations

1-A   2-C   3-B   4-D   5-D   6-C   7-D   8-A   9-A   10-B

Duties of the insured Condition found in property policies that explains the insured's responsibilities after a loss occurs.

Obligations of the insurance company Condition found in property policies that explains the insurer's responsibilities after a loss occurs.

Mortgagee rights Specifies the rights and duties of the mortgagee under the policy.

Proof of loss Forms completed by an insured after a loss that provides an official inventory of damages.

Notice of claim When the insured notifies the insurance company of a loss.

Appraisal Policy condition that outlines a procedure for when the insured and insurer disagree on the amount of a loss. The insured and the insurer each select an appraiser. The two appraisers select an umpire. If the appraisers cannot agree on the amount of the loss, the umpire is consulted. The amount agreed to by any two of the three parties is the amount paid for the loss.

The cost for the umpire is shared. The cost for the appraiser is borne by each party respectively.

Other Insurance Provision Policy condition that sets out how any other insurance that applies to the same loss will affect reimbursement under the policy.

Assignment Condition in insurance policies that specifies that the policy cannot be transferred to another unless the company consents to the transfer in writing.

Subrogation The transfer to the insurance company of the insured's right to collect damages from another party.

Elements of a contract
(1) Offer and Acceptance An application or premium quotation may constitute an offer. An offer may be terminated by making a counter offer. There is no requirement that the contract be in writing.

(2) Consideration is thing of value which each party gives to the other. The company's consideration is a promise to indemnify the insured in the event of a loss. The insured's consideration is the premium or the promise to pay the premium and an agreement to abide by the conditions of the contract.

(3) Competent Parties Both parties to the contract must be competent and capable of entering into a contract in the eyes of the law.

(4) Legal Purpose Contracts must have legal object and cannot be for an illegal activity or an immoral purpose.

Sources of insurability information include producer applications, motor vehicle reports (MVR), consumer credit companies, and financial sources such as Dun and Bradstreet.

1. Following a loss, the insured does NOT have a duty to

A. Protect the property from further damage
B. Give prompt notice of claim to the insurer
C. Determine the valuation method to be used
D. Submit to an examination under oath if required

2. Duties of the insured after a loss do NOT include

A. Abandoning the property to the insurer
B. Making an inventory of damaged property
C. Allowing the insurer to inspect the property
D. Assisting the insurer in claims investigation

3. In event of a loss, valuation methods by the insurance company would NOT include

A. Appraisal
B. Arbitration
C. Actual cash value
D. Replacement cost

4. As loss payee, the mortgagee

A. Is expected to forfeit any rights to protect the property
B. Cannot file proof of loss if the insured fails to file proof of loss
C. Is expected to pay the premium if the insured fails to make premium payment
D. Cannot assign all mortgagee rights to the insurance company and eliminate the mortgagee's interest

5. When the insured and insurer disagree on the amount of a loss, the appraisal process involves

A. The court
B. Three adjusters
C. Two adjusters and an umpire
D. Two appraisers and an umpire

6. The assignment condition specifies that in the event of the death of the named insured, the rights and duties under the policy are transferred to the

A. IRS
B. Insured's heirs
C. Insured's estate
D. Insured's legal representative

7. The insurer's right to recover against a negligent third party is obtained through the right of

A. Salvage
B. Arbitration
C. Subrogation
D. Assignment

8. A legally binding contract requires offer and acceptance. What happens when a counter offer is made?

A. The counter offer is NOT valid
B. The original offer is terminated
C. The original offer remains valid
D. Acceptance can be made on the original offer

9. Elements of a legally binding contract would NOT include

A. Capacity
B. Consideration
C. Legal purpose
D. Competent parties

10. The Fair Credit Reporting Act

A. Imposes a maximum criminal penalty of up to 5 years in prison for fraudulent use of consumer information
B. Does not give the consumer the right to know what was in the report
C. Was established to protect creditors from unfair and inaccurate information
D. Requires the investigative consumer report to advise the consumer in writing within 3 days after the report is requested

1-C   2-A   3-B   4-C   5-D

6-D   7-C   8-B   9-A   10-D

Privacy Protection (Gramm Leach Bliley)
Under the *GLB*, financial institutions must provide their clients a privacy notice that explains what information the company gathers about the client, where this information is shared, and how the company safeguards that information.

This privacy notice must be given to the client prior to entering into an agreement to do business. The privacy notice must also explain to the customer the opportunity to 'opt-out'.

"Opting-out" means that the client can say "no" to allowing their information to be shared with affiliated parties.

Policy Application form contains the pertinent information when applying for insurance coverage.

Premium Payments Monthly, quarterly, semi-annually or annually.

Effective dates of coverage Generally a policy begins and expires at 12:01 a.m. Standard Time on the date and location indicated in the declarations.

Terrorism Risk Insurance Act (TRIA)
TRIA is federal program that provides up to $100 billion in the event of terrorism attack. The Terrorism Risk Insurance Program Reauthorization Act of December 26, 2007 extended the program by seven years through December 31, 2014.

The Act's purposes are to address market disruptions, ensure the continued widespread availability and affordability of commercial property and casualty insurance for terrorism risk, and to allow for a transition period for the private markets to stabilize and build capacity while preserving state insurance regulation and consumer protections.

These 3 persons of the federal government make up the entity who certifies an act as terrorism: the Attorney General, Secretary of State, and Secretary of Treasury.

To qualify as a certified act under TRIA, the act must be a violent act committed by someone resulting in damage in the US or to a US air carrier or ship, and result in aggregate losses in excess of $100 million.

Coverage must be offered by endorsement to all commercial policyholders.

Cancellation Termination of an insurance policy by the insured or the insurance company during the policy period.

If the policy is **canceled by the insured**, the insured may pay to the company the customary **short rates** and costs of action.

If the policy is **canceled by the insurance company**, the insurer may retain only the **pro rata premium**.

If the policy is canceled on the effective date by either the insurance company or the insured, it is called **flat cancellation**.

Nonrenewal Decision made by an insured or insurance company to not continue coverage for another policy period after the current policy period expires.

Additional (supplementary) payments Provide extra coverage over and above the insured's limit of liability. Commonly included are defense costs, first aid expenses, bond premiums, and post judgment interest.

Arbitration A policy condition used to resolve other areas of disagreement besides those regarding the value of a loss.

Professional designations Evidence that a person has successfully completed a course of study, e.g. CPCU, CLU, CFP, LUTCF.

1. The Gramm Leach Bliley (GLB) Act does NOT require financial institutions to

A. Provide their clients a privacy notice
B. Explain to the customer the opportunity to "opt-out"
C. Explain what information the company gathers about the client
D. Disclose the company's financial statements

2. Generally a policy begins and expires at

A. 12:01 a.m. Pacific
B. 12:01 a.m. Central
C. 12:01 a.m. Eastern
D. 12:01 a.m. Standard

3. The Terrorism Risk Insurance Act requires coverage to be offered to all

A. Personal property policyholders
B. Property and casualty policyholders
C. Commercial property and casualty policyholders
D. Life, Health, property and casualty policyholders

4. The entity which certifies the act as terrorism is the

A. President
B. U.S. Senate
C. U.S. Congress
D. Federal government

5. All of the following must certify the act as terrorism EXCEPT

A. Vice-President
B. Secretary of State
C. Attorney General
D. Secretary of Treasury

6. To qualify as a certified act under TRIA, the act must result in aggregate losses in excess of

A. $100 million
B. $150 million
C. $200 million
D. $250 million

7. When the insurance company cancels an insurance policy, the return premium is

A. A flat cancellation
B. On a pro rata basis
C. On a short rate basis
D. A full premium refund

8. When an insured requests cancellation, the return premium is usually

A. A flat cancellation
B. On a pro rata basis
C. On a short rate basis
D. A full premium refund

9. If the insured and insurer disagree concerning any matter other than the value of a loss, the matter is resolved using the process of

A. Appraisal
B. Mediation
C. Arbitration
D. Adjustment

10. Which of the following is NOT a professional insurance designation?

A. CFP
B. CPA
C. CPCU
D. LUTCF

1-D   2-D   3-C   4-D   5-A   6-A   7-B   8-C   9-C   10-B

PROPERTY INSURANCE - TYPES OF PROPERTY POLICIES

I. DWELLING AND CONTENTS
(2002 DP forms)

Characteristics
The Dwelling Policy provides coverage for risks which may not qualify for the Homeowner Policy.

Dwelling policies provides property coverage only. However, liability and medical payments can be covered under a separate liability policy or added by endorsement. There is no theft coverage without endorsement. Exception: theft on DP-3 building items is provided.

The owner of the dwelling may or may not occupy the dwelling and still be eligible for dwelling insurance.

Eligible property
The covered dwelling may be a townhouse, row house, vacation home or a dwelling under construction. Permanently located mobile homes can only use the basic form.

A landlord could use the dwelling policy to cover a residence rented to others. The dwelling may have up to four apartments and be occupied by no more than five roomers or boarders.

A limited group of incidental service business and professional occupancies are permitted such as beauty parlors and professional offices. These businesses must be conducted by the insured and can have no more than two people working on the premises at any one time.

Land is excluded.

Insured persons
The named insured is covered and the named insured's spouse is covered if the spouse lives in the same household.

Property Coverages
The Dwelling Policy has 5 separate property coverages lettered A, B, C, D, and E.

COVERAGE A - DWELLING
Coverage for the dwelling described in the policy, including:
- any additions in contact with the dwelling.
- materials and supplies located on or next to the described location and intended for use in construction, alterations or repair of the dwelling.
- building & outdoor equipment used for the service of & located on the premises.

COVERAGE B - OTHER STRUCTURES
- Coverage for structures on the premises set apart from the dwelling by a clear space such as garages and swimming pools.

COVERAGE C - PERSONAL PROPERTY
- Coverage on personal property owned or used by the insured and usual and incidental to the occupancy of a dwelling. Personal property owned by a guest or servant is covered after a loss at the insured's request.
- Coverage on personal property is Actual Cash Value, with no option for Replacement Cost coverage.
- Coverage at a new residence location applies for 30 days.
- Excludes: animals, birds, fish, aircraft, motor vehicles and boats.
- Covers rowboats and canoes at the premises only.

COVERAGE D - FAIR RENTAL VALUE
Provides for the loss of rental income when a loss under Coverages A, B, or C makes property that is rented or held for rental "unfit for normal use".

COVERAGE E - ADDITIONAL LIVING EXPENSE
Applies to the necessary increase in living expenses incurred by the insured in order to continue as nearly as practicable the normal standard of living of his/her household following loss by an insured peril.

1. The Dwelling Policy covers

A. Property coverage only
B. Liability payments only
C. Owner-occupied dwellings only
D. Medical payments without endorsement

2. A Dwelling policy would NOT cover

A. Certain incidental business and professional occupancies
B. A dwelling with more than four apartments
C. A townhouse or row house
D. A dwelling under construction

3. Dwelling policies could NOT be used to insure

A. Mobile homes
B. Vacation homes
C. A dwelling with more than five boarders
D. The owner of a home that is rented to tenants

4. Property eligible for the Dwelling Policy may include

A. Land
B. Dwellings having up to four apartments
C. Dwellings having up to five apartments
D. Dwellings occupied by no more than six roomers or boarders

5. The Dwelling Policy would NOT cover an incidental business such as a

A. Law office with two employees
B. Beauty parlor operated by the insured
C. Sole-proprietor photography business
D. Woodworking business in the garage

6. Insured persons under the Dwelling Policy include

A. Only the named insured
B. An employee of the named insured
C. The named insured's spouse even though separated
D. The named insured's spouse only while living in the same household

7. Coverage A – Dwelling under the Dwelling Policy does NOT cover

A. Detached garages
B. Structures attached to the dwelling
C. Building and outdoor equipment used to service the dwelling
D. Materials and supplies located on or next to the residence premises used to construct, alter or repair the dwelling

8. Personal property coverage under the Dwelling Policy is paid on what basis?

A. Historical cost
B. Fair market value
C. Replacement cost
D. Actual cash value

9. Personal property coverage under the Dwelling Policy at a new residence location applies for:

A. 10 days
B. 15 days
C. 30 days
D. 45 days

10. Coverage C – Personal Property under the Dwelling Policy excludes or limits all of the following property EXCEPT

A. Watercraft
B. Coins and currency
C. Animals, birds and fish
D. Rowboats and canoes located on the premises

1-A   2-B   3-C   4-C   5-D   6-D   7-A   8-D   9-C   10-D

Coverage Forms - Perils insured against

BASIC FORM DWELLING POLICY DP-1

1. Provides coverage on a named peril basis. Losses are paid actual cash value. It covers fire, lightning, and internal explosion.

2. The (9) **Extended Coverage Perils (EC)** for direct loss coverage can be added for an additional premium.

The EC provision broadens coverage but does not increase the limit of the policy.

EC Memory Key: "W. C. SHAVVER"
Wind, Civil commotion, Smoke, Hail, Aircraft, Vehicles, Volcanic eruption, Explosion and Riot

Notice: The extended coverage perils do not include theft or collapse.

Smoke includes puffback (the emission of smoke, soot, fumes or vapors from a boiler or furnace).

Vehicle damage does not cover damage by a vehicle owned or operated by the insured or a resident of the household.

Volcanic eruption covers volcanic blast, airborne shock waves, ash, dust or lava flow, fire, and explosion resulting from volcanic eruption. It excludes loss caused by earthquake, land tremors, landslide, mudflow and other earth movement. Multiple volcanic eruptions within a 72 hour period are considered as one occurrence.

Vandalism or Malicious Mischief coverage can be added for an additional premium. It excludes pilferage, theft or burglary. Loss is not covered if the building has been vacant for over 60 days.

Other Coverages of the Basic Form include:
Other structures up to 10% of A; Debris removal, Property removed, Reasonable repairs, Improvements, alterations, and additions up to 10% of C, Fire department service charges up to $500 (no deductible); Worldwide coverage of 10% of C; and Rental value of 20% of A.

BROAD FORM DWELLING POLICY DP-2

1. Broad Form DP-2 provides replacement cost coverage on the dwellings & buildings on a **"named peril"** basis. Contents are actual cash value.

2. The Broad Form DP 2 adds these perils:
- Damage by burglars
- Falling objects
- Weight of ice and snow
- Accidental discharge or overflow of water or steam
- Sudden and accidental tearing apart, cracking, burning or bulging from within a plumbing system
- Freezing of plumbing
- Fireplace smoke
- Artificially generated electrical current.

Other Coverages includes all those in DP1 plus:
- Collapse
- Glass or Safety Glazing Material
- Ordinance or law
- Trees, shrubs, plants or lawns up to 5% of A; $500 maximum per tree, shrub.

SPECIAL FORM DWELLING POLICY DP-3

Special Form DP 3 provides replacement cost coverage on the dwelling and other structures on an **"open-peril"** basis which covers all risks of direct physical loss unless specifically excluded. Contents are on a named peril basis.

Uninsurable (excluded) losses under the open-peril insuring agreement include damage caused by rust, mold, wear and tear, birds, insects, vermin, domestic animals, and continuous or repeated seepage from water systems.

1. The Basic Dwelling Form DP-1 does NOT cover

A. Fire
B. Lightning
C. Falling objects
D. Internal explosion

2. The Dwelling Form Basic DP-1 "extended coverage perils" would NOT include

A. Aircraft
B. Collapse
C. Vehicles
D. Windstorm

3. Volcanic eruption under the Dwelling Policy does NOT cover

A. Land tremors
B. Volcanic blast
C. Airborne shock waves
D. Ash, dust and lava flow

4. Multiple volcanic eruptions within what period of time are considered as one occurrence?

A. 24 hours
B. 48 hours
C. 72 hours
D. 96 hours

5. Vandalism and malicious mischief does not cover damage to a building vacant more than

A. 15 consecutive days
B. 30 consecutive days
C. 45 consecutive days
D. 60 consecutive days

6. The Dwelling Broad Form DP 2 provides coverage on

A. An open-peril basis on buildings
B. A replacement cost basis for contents
C. A named peril basis on the dwellings
D. A replacement cost basis for dwellings

7. The Dwelling Broad Form DP-2 does NOT cover

A. Intentional loss
B. Fireplace smoke
C. Damage by burglars
D. Freezing of plumbing

8. The Other Coverages of the Dwelling Basic Form includes trees, shrubs, plants or lawns up to what maximum amount per tree or shrub?

A. $250
B. $500
C. $750
D. $1,000

9. Which of the following Dwelling Forms provides coverage for risk of direct physical loss unless the loss is excluded?

A. Dwelling Policy Basic Form
B. Dwelling Policy Broad Form
C. Dwelling Policy Special Form
D. Dwelling Policy Theft Coverage

10. The Dwelling Policy Special Form includes

A. Mold, wet or dry rot
B. Settling, shrinking, bulging or expansion
C. Continuous or repeated seepage from water systems
D. Damage caused by burglars in an attempt to steal property

1-C   2-B   3-A   4-C   5-D   6-C   7-A   8-B   9-C   10-D

General exclusions

Exclusions applicable to all dwelling forms:
Ordinance or law, earth movement, water damage,
power failure, neglect, war, nuclear hazard,
intentional loss, and governmental action.

Conditions

The **"Other Insurance"** clause of Dwelling
Property forms provides for distributing insurance
among two or more insurers on a pro-rata basis.

Under the **"Loss Payment"** condition, the loss will
be paid within 30 days following agreement with the
insured.

"Pair and set clause" In case of loss to a pair or set
the insurer may elect to:
1. Repair or replace any part to restore the pair or set
to its value before the loss; or
2. Pay the difference between actual cash value of
the property before and after the loss.

The **"Our Option"** condition grants the insurer the
right to repair or replace damaged property within 30
days after receiving the statement of loss.

Selected endorsements

Automatic increase in insurance
An endorsement used to provide an annual increase
of 4%, 6%, or 8% in coverage A of the dwelling
property forms.

Broad theft coverage
The theft endorsement covers theft of personal
property for any dwelling policy written on a
dwelling, co-op, or condominium unit that is owner-
occupied, or a tenant in an apartment.

Dwelling under construction
This endorsement insures the named insured while
the dwelling is under construction. The limit of
liability is a percentage of the value of the partially
completed home at any given time.

27

1. The Dwelling Special Form DP-3 covers

A. Earth movement
B. Water damage
C. Power failure
D. Volcanic eruption

2. The "Other Insurance" clause provides for distributing insurance among two or more insurers on a

A. Pro-rata basis
B. Flat rate basis
C. Short rate basis
D. Excess over basis

3. Following agreement with the insurer, a loss will be paid within how many days under the "Loss Payment" condition?

A. 15 days
B. 20 days
C. 30 days
D. 45 days

4. Mary owns a matching pair of unique hand-blown vases worth $200. Individually the vases are worth $75 each. One of the vases is destroyed. How much will the insurance company pay under the "pair and set clause?"

A. $75
B. $125
C. $150
D. $200

5. Tom has a pair of matching engraved ivory handled pistols from Italy worth $1,200. Individually the pistols are worth $500. One of the pistols is destroyed. How much will the insurance company pay under the "pair and set" clause?"

A. $500
B. $700
C. $1,000
D. $1,200

6. Mary has a pair of earrings worth $200. Individually the earrings are worth $100. One of the earrings is destroyed. How much will the insurance company pay under the "pair and set" clause?"

A. Nothing
B. $50
C. $100
D. $200

7. The insurer has the right to repair or replace damaged property within how many days after receiving the statement of loss?

A. 30 days
B. 60 days
C. 90 days
D. 120 days

8. During a period of increasing prices due to inflation, an insured would need which endorsement to protect against being underinsured at the time of loss?

A. Price protection endorsement
B. Construction cost endorsement
C. Actual cash value endorsement
D. Automatic increase in insurance endorsement

9. The theft endorsement of the Dwelling Policy covers theft of

A. Aircraft
B. Hovercraft
C. Automobiles
D. Personal property

10. The limit of liability under the Dwelling Under Construction Endorsement is

A. Appraised value
B. Replacement cost
C. Actual cash value
D. A percentage of the value of the partially completed home at any given time.

1-D   2-A   3-C   4-B   5-B   6-C   7-A   8-D   9-D   10-D

Homeowners (HO Forms)

Coverage	HO-2 Homeowners	HO-3 Homeowners	HO-5 Comprehensive	HO-8 Modified	HO-4 Tenants	HO-6 Condominium
A. Dwelling	Policy Limit	Policy Limit	Policy Limit	Policy Limit	N/A	$1,000
B. Other Structures						
1-2 Family	10% of A	10% of A	10% of A	10% of A	N/A	N/A
3-4 Family	5% of A	5% of A	5% of A	5% of A		
C. Personal Property						
1-2 Family	50% of A	50% of A	50% of A	50% of A	Primary Limit	Primary Limit
3 Family	30% of A	30% of A	30% of A	30% of A		
4 Family	25% of A	25% of A	25% of A	25% of A		
D. Loss of Use	30% of A	30% of A	30% of A	10% of A	30% of C	50% of C
Dwelling Property Perils	Broad	Special	Special	Basic	N/A	Limited
Personal Property Perils	Broad	Broad	Special	Basic	Broad	Broad
Fire	X	X		X	X	X
Lightning	X	X		X	X	X
Windstorm or Hail	X	X		X	X	X
Explosion	X	X		X	X	X
Riot or Civil Commotion	X	X		X	X	X
Aircraft	X	X		X	X	X
Vehicles	X	X		X	X	X
Smoke	X	X		X	X	X
Vandalism & Malicious Mischief	X	X		X	X	X
Theft	X	X		X	X	X
Volcanic Eruption	X	X		X	X	X
Falling Objects	X	X			X	X
Weight of Ice, Snow, or Sleet	X	X			X	X
Discharge of Water or Steam	X	X			X	X
Sudden, Accidental Rupture	X	X			X	X
Freezing of Plumbing & Related Systems	X	X			X	X
Artificially Generated Electrical Current	X	X			X	X

The HO-5 is only for newer, high value, well-maintained homes.
The HO-8 is for older homes whose market value is considerably less than the cost to rebuild them.
The HO-4 is "renter's insurance" for tenant's personal property.
The HO-6 is for condominium owners.

The Basic and Broad perils are on a "named peril" basis. The Special perils are an "open peril" basis.

1. Which Homeowners Policy provides Broad peril coverage on both the dwelling and personal property?

A. HO-2
B. HO-3
C. HO-4
D. HO-5

2. The Homeowners Policy providing special peril coverage on the dwelling and broad peril coverage on personal property is

A. HO-2
B. HO-3
C. HO-4
D. HO-5

3. The HO-5 Comprehensive Form provides coverage on what basis on both the dwelling and personal property?

A. Broad
B. Limited
C. Special
D. Primary

4. Which Homeowners Policy provides basic peril coverage on both the dwelling and personal property?

A. HO-4
B. HO-5
C. HO-6
D. HO-8

5. The tenants HO-4 Form does NOT provide coverage for the dwelling and other structures but covers personal property on a

A. Broad basis
B. Limited basis
C. Special basis
D. Primary basis

6. Which of the following Homeowner Policies would be most likely written for newer, well maintained, higher value homes on an open peril basis for both property and contents?

A. HO-4
B. HO-5
C. HO-6
D. HO-8

7. An agent wanting to write insurance for an older home whose market value is considerably less than the cost to rebuild it would use which Homeowners Policy?

A. HO-4
B. HO-5
C. HO-6
D. HO-8

8. The HO-4 is commonly known as

A. Renter's insurance
C. Modified insurance
B. Condominium insurance
D. Comprehensive insurance

9. The form used by a condominium owner would be the

A. HO-4
B. HO-5
C. HO-6
D. HO-8

10. Special perils are on what basis?

A. Open peril
B. Named peril
C. Primary peril
D. Limited peril

1-A   2-B   3-C   4-D   5-A   6-B   7-D   8-A   9-C   10-A

Homeowners Policy
A homeowners policy eliminates gaps in coverage because it contains both property (Section I) and liability (Section II) coverages. It establishes minimums on both the dwelling and its contents.

The cost is less than if the coverages were purchased separately and it provides one policy with one premium rather than a number of policies. It does NOT provide great flexibility.

Eligible Property
Must be owner/renter occupied and the home cannot contain more than 4 families. One additional family or not more than two roomers or boarders are allowed per family.

Farms are not eligible. Mobile homes are covered by endorsement. Seasonal/secondary homes and dwellings under construction are eligible.

Insured Persons
The definition of "insured" means you and the following residents of your household:

a. Your relatives (by blood, marriage or adoption) or any other person under age 21 who is in the care of any person named above (foster child, ward);

b. A student enrolled in school full time, who was a resident of your household before moving out to attend school provided the student is under the age of: 24 and your relative; or 21 and in your care or the care of your relatives.

c. Under Section II: Any person or organization legally responsible for animals or watercraft which are owned by you or persons above. They are not insured in the course of any business, or without the permission of the owner.

An employee is an insured while operating a "motor vehicle" or trailer/semitrailer being carried on, towed by or hitched for towing by the vehicle as well as any other persons using the vehicle on an "insured location" with your consent.

Insured Location
The following are considered insured premises: residence premises, vacant land owned, premises occasionally rented to the insured (wedding hall, picnic grove), cemetery plots or burial vaults, and unowned premises where the insured temporarily resides (hotel, motel, campground).

Business property is NOT considered insured premises.

SECTION I – PROPERTY COVERAGES

Section I of the homeowners policy has 4 separate property coverages lettered A, B, C, and D.

Coverage A – Dwelling
Covers the dwelling, including structures attached to the dwelling and materials and supplies located on or next to the "residence premises" used to construct, alter or repair the dwelling or other structures on the "residence premises".

The HO-3 provides open-perils coverage on the dwelling and named peril coverage on the contents.

The HO-4 Tenants form is unique because it does not provide coverage for real property, i.e. the dwelling and buildings.

The HO-5 Comprehensive form provides open-perils coverage on both the dwelling and contents.

The HO-6 Condominium form includes limited coverage of $1,000 for alterations, appliances, fixtures, and improvements that are part of the building.

The HO-8 Modified form is for older homes whose market value is considerably less than the cost to rebuild them. It only provides the Basic perils for the dwelling and personal property.

Coverage B – Other Structures
Covers buildings on the residence premises that are set apart from the dwelling by clear space. It excludes other structures used for business, but covers the other structure when rented to someone as a private passenger garage.

1. A Homeowners Policy does NOT

A. Provide one policy with one premium
B. Contain both property and liability coverage
C. Establish minimums on dwelling and contents
D. Provide great flexibility in covering non-conforming property

2. Eligible property under the Homeowners Policy

A. Excludes additional families
B. May contain more than 4 families
C. Does not require the dwelling to be owner/renter occupied
D. Does not allow more than two roomers or boarders per family

3. The Homeowners Policy would NOT cover

A. Farms
B. Mobile homes by endorsement
C. Seasonal and secondary homes
D. Dwellings under construction

4. Under the Homeowners '00 policies, "Insured" does NOT mean

A. You
B. Employees
C. Other persons under the age of 21 and in the care of you
D. Residents of your household who are your relatives

5. The Homeowners Policy will insure a student who was a resident relative of your household before moving out to attend school and who is enrolled full time and under age

A. 18
B. 21
C. 24
D. 27

6. An "Insured location" under the Homeowners '00 policies can be all of the following EXCEPT

A. The residence premises
B. Premises rented to an insured for business use
C. Individual or family cemetery plots or burial vaults of an insured
D. Vacant land, other than farm land, owned by or rented to an insured

7. The HO-4 Tenants Form is unique because it does NOT provide coverage for

A. Liability
B. Real property
C. Personal property
D. Medical payments

8. The HO-6 Condominium Form includes limited coverage for

A. Auto liability
B. Other structures
C. Professional liability
D. Alterations, appliances, fixtures, and improvements that are part of the building

9. The HO-8 Modified form is for

A. Condominiums
B. Newer, high-value, well maintained homes
C. Open peril coverage on dwelling and personal property
D. Older homes whose market value is considerably less than the cost to rebuild them

10. Coverage B – Other Structures of the Homeowners Policy EXCLUDES

A. A tool shed
B. Structures used for business
C. Buildings set apart from the dwelling by clear space
D. A garage rented to someone as a private passenger garage

1-D   2-D   3-A   4-B   5-C   6-B   7-B   8-D   9-D   10-B

Coverage C – Personal Property

The off-premises coverage of the Homeowners Forms applies on a world-wide basis and is the same limit at premises as away from premises.

Coverage C provides full coverage for property moved to a temporary residence if the residence premises is unfit to live in or store property, or is being repaired, renovated or rebuilt.

It provides full coverage for 30 days in a newly acquired principal residence.

Special Limits

The internal limits of the Homeowners Policy include $200 limit of money and bullion, $1500 limit on securities, manuscripts and valuable papers, $1500 on watercraft, including trailers, furnishings, equipment and outboard engines or motors, $1500 on trailers or semitrailers not used with watercraft, $1500 for electronic apparatus and accessories while it is in or upon on a motor vehicle.

Property Used for Business Purposes

$2500 for property on the residence premises, e.g., business computer, $500 for property away from the residence premises, and $1500 for electronic apparatus and accessories used primarily for business while away from the residence premises and not in or upon a motor vehicle.

Theft Coverage. Theft coverage on contents is included in homeowners and is defined as: "Theft, including attempted theft or loss of property from a known location when it is likely that the property has been stolen."

Theft coverage under Homeowners does not include theft from that part of the dwelling rented to others, theft in a dwelling under construction or theft committed by an insured.

The theft coverage of the Homeowners Forms applies both on and off premises.

Special Limits for Loss by Theft

The homeowners forms provide a special limitation for loss by theft, misplacing or losing of jewelry, watches, furs, precious and semi-precious stones to $1,500 per loss. The limit for loss by theft, misplacing or losing of firearms and related equipment is $2500. Theft of silverware, goldware, platinumware and pewterware is limited to $2500. There are no internal limits for glassware.

Excluded Property

Animals, birds or fish, motor vehicles, aircraft, hovercraft, property of unrelated roomers and boarders, property in an apartment regularly rented to others, business data, credit cards, electronic fund transfer cards, and water or steam.

Coverage D – Loss of Use

Additional Living Expense provides payment for any necessary increase in living expenses incurred so that a household can maintain its normal standard of living when a covered property loss makes the residence premises unfit to live in.

Fair Rental Value covers the fair rental value of premises rented to others or held for rental, less any expenses that do not continue while it is not fit to live in.

Additional Coverages

The homeowners policy includes Debris Removal, Reasonable Repairs, Trees, Shrubs And Other Plants ($500 limit per tree, shrub or plant), Fire Department Service Charge, Property Removed, Credit Card, Fund Transfer Card, Forgery, and Counterfeit Money, Loss Assessment, Collapse, Glass of Safety Glazing material, Landlord's Furnishings, Ordinance Or Law and Grave Markers ($5000).

Exclusions

Loss caused directly or indirectly by earth movement, water damage, power failure, neglect, war, nuclear hazard, intentional loss or governmental action (the destruction, confiscation or seizure of property by order of any governmental or public authority) is excluded.

1. Full coverage for personal property when moved to a temporary residence is NOT covered if the premises is being

A. Rebuilt
B. Repaired
C. Renovated
D. Regularly rented to others

2. For a newly acquired principal residence, Coverage C – Personal Property provides full coverage for

A. 15 days
B. 30 days
C. 45 days
D. 60 days

3. The internal limits for money and bullion under the Homeowners Policy is

A. $200
B. $250
C. $300
D. $500

4. Property used for business purposes on the residence premises is limited to

A. $1,000
B. $1,500
C. $2,000
D. $2,500

5. Theft coverage under the Homeowners Policy includes

A. Theft committed by an insured
B. Theft in a dwelling under construction
C. Theft of personal property off premises
D. Theft from that part of a dwelling rented to others

6. Theft of firearms and related equipment is limited to

A. $1,000
B. $1,500
C. $2,000
D. $2,500

7. Covered property under the Homeowners includes

A. Animals, birds or fish
B. Furniture, appliances, and clothing
C. Motor vehicles, aircraft, and hovercraft
D. Property of unrelated roomers and boarders

8. "Loss of Use" under the Homeowners is NOT available if the

A. Government confiscates or seizes the dwelling
B. The owner-occupant can't live in the dwelling
C. The owner-occupant is ordered by a civil authority to move because of covered damage to a neighboring premises
D. The owner-occupant can't rent the portion of the dwelling rented to others

9. The Homeowners Policy does NOT cover

A. Collapse
B. Debris removal
C. Earth movement
D. Fire department service charge

10. The Homeowners Policy EXCLUDES

A. Forgery
B. Power failure
C. Grave markers
D. Counterfeit money

1-D   2-B   3-A   4-D   5-C   6-D   7-B   8-A   9-C   10-B

Section I - Conditions

Under Section I (property) of Homeowners '00 Policy, the insured must submit a statement of loss within 60 days after the insurer's request. The insured has 2 years to bring legal action against the insurer.

Replacement Cost. The replacement cost extension of the homeowners requires the insured to actually replace or repair the loss if the loss is greater than $2500. The insured must carry at least 80% of replacement cost to avoid a penalty on a partial loss.

Loss Payment. Losses will be payable 60 days after the insurer receives proof of loss.

Volcanic Eruption Period. One or more volcanic eruptions that occur within a 72 hour period will be considered as one volcanic eruption.

SECTION II – LIABILITY COVERAGES

Coverage E -- Personal liability

The insurer will pay up to the limit of liability of the policy all sums which the insured becomes legally obligated to pay because of bodily injury or property damage. It includes suit brought by one insured against another insured under the same policy.

Coverage E (liability) of the CPL excludes coverage for property damage to property owned by the insured, property rented on a short-term basis for use by the insured, and property borrowed which is in the care, custody or control of the insured. It covers bodily injury due to premises liability.

Coverage F -- Medical payments to others

Coverage F of the Homeowners provides medical payments which are non-liability payments covering medical expenses incurred within three years from the date of accident causing bodily injury.

It provides medical payments even though the insured is not legally liable. Medical Expenses includes reasonable charges for medical, surgical, x-ray, dental, ambulance, hospital, professional nursing, prosthetic devices and funeral services.

It excludes: residence employees away from the premises, workers compensation, nuclear explosion, and persons residing on premises. NOTE: There are no medical payments to the named insured, a roomer, or to a tenant living in portion of the insured residence.

Both Coverage E (liability) and Coverage F (medical payments) EXCLUDE: intentional injury, business pursuits, professional services, uninsured premises, war, communicable disease, sexual molestation, corporal punishment or physical or mental abuse or controlled substances other than legitimate use of prescription drugs.

Section II - Additional coverages

In addition to the limits of liability, the Homeowners pays: 1) Claim Expense (loss of earnings up to $250/day), 2) First Aid Expense to others, 3) Loss Assessment and 4) Damage To Property Of Others up to $1,000 per occurrence regardless of legal liability. This is a non-liability coverage just as medical payments are non-liability payments.

Section II - Conditions

Section II conditions state that this insurance is excess over other valid and collectible insurance.

Section II - Exclusions

Classes of property specifically excluded from coverage are motorized vehicles licensed for road use, aircraft liability, hovercraft liability, and watercraft liability.

1. Under Section I (property) of the Homeowners Policy, the insured must submit a statement of loss within how many days after the insurer's request?

A. 30 days
B. 60 days
C. 90 days
D. 120 days

2. The insured has how many years to bring legal action against the insurer?

A. 2 years
B. 3 years
C. 4 years
D. 5 years

3. The insured must carry what percent of replacement cost to avoid a penalty on a partial loss?

A. 50%
B. 75%
C. 80%
D. 100%

4. Under the loss payment condition of the Homeowners Policy, losses will be payable how many days after the insurer receives proof of loss?

A. 15 days
B. 30 days
C. 45 days
D. 60 days

5. One or more volcanic eruptions that occur within what period of time will be considered as one volcanic eruption?

A. 24 hours
B. 48 hours
C. 72 hours
D. 96 hours

6. Liability coverage under the Homeowners covers

A. Damage to property owned by the insured
B. Property rented on a short-term basis for use by the insured
C. Property borrowed which is in the care, custody or control of the insured
D. Sums which the insured is legally obligated to pay because of bodily injury or property damage

7. Under a Homeowners '00 Policy, medical payments coverage pays expenses incurred for what maximum period of time from the date of the accident?

A. 1 year
B. 3 years
C. 5 years
D. Indefinite

8. Personal Liability under the Homeowners program covers

A. Expected or intended injury
B. Defense costs and prejudgment interest
C. Bodily injury or property damage arising out of or in connection with a business
D. Bodily injury or property damage arising out of the rendering of or failure to render professional services

9. Additional coverages under the homeowners pays for Damage To Property of Others up to

A. $1,000 per occurrence
B. $1,500 per occurrence
C. $2000 per occurrence
D. $2,500 per occurrence

10. Section II of the Homeowners states that this insurance is

A. Pro-rated with other insurance
B. Primary in relation to other insurance
C. Excess over other valid and collectible insurance
D. Not applicable if other valid and collectible insurance is available

1-B   2-A   3-C   4-D   5-C   6-D   7-B   8-B   9-A   10-C

HOMEOWNERS ENDORSEMENTS

SECTION I

Scheduled personal property.
An endorsement providing open-peril property coverage on nine different classes of scheduled property. In effect, it is a separate inland marine contract.

Jewelry, furs, cameras, projectors, films and equipment, musical instruments, silverware, golfer's equipment, fine arts, postage stamps and rare and current coins scheduled under a homeowners policy are covered on an open peril basis with no deductible.

However, when a scheduled personal property endorsement is written with a homeowners policy no coverage then exists under the homeowner contract on those specifically insured, scheduled items.

Personal property replacement cost.
Converts the coverage on personal property to a replacement cost basis.

Permitted incidental occupancies.
Designed for the situation in which the insured is engaged in a business activity on the residence premises that falls within the scope of the permitted incidental occupancies.

Home day care.
Covers the home day care business conducted by an insured on the premises. The premium is determined by the number of children under care.

Earthquake.
Covers earthquakes, landslides, volcanic eruptions and earth movements that occur within a 72 hour period as if they were a single loss. The deductible that applies to the earthquake endorsement must be at least $250.

SECTION II

Watercraft.
Covers scheduled watercraft for liability with inboard or inboard-outdrive engines, watercraft up to 26 feet long with outboard motors in excess of 25 HP, or any sailing vessel in excess of 26 feet

Business pursuits endorsement.
Provides liability coverage for an insured as an employee in the course of an occupation in which the insured is not an owner or partner such as school teachers, clerical office employees and sales persons.

Personal injury.
Includes coverage for false arrest, detention, imprisonment, or malicious prosecution, libel, slander, defamation, or violation of the right of privacy, wrongful entry or eviction, or other invasion of the right of private occupancy.

SECTIONS I AND II

Limited Fungi, Wet or Dry Rot, or Bacteria Coverage.
Covers property damage and liability losses from fungi (including mold or mildew), wet or dry rot, or bacteria. It is available on forms HO-3 and HO-5.

The endorsement covers liability resulting from contact with mold, the cost to remove mold from covered property, and the cost to tear out and replace any part of the building to gain access to the mold. It excludes fungi that are part of a product intended for consumption.

1. Personal property scheduled under the personal property endorsement is covered on

A. An open peril basis with no deductible
B. A named peril basis with no deductible
C. An all risk basis subject to a deductible
D. A named peril basis subject to a deductible

2. The personal property replacement cost endorsement excludes articles that are not easily replaced, but would cover

A. Fine art
B. Furniture
C. Antiques
D. Paintings

3. Even though a beauty parlor or barbershop conducted on the residence premises is a business activity, it can be covered under the

A. Inland marine policy
B. Personal articles floater
C. Scheduled personal property endorsement
D. Permitted incidental occupancies endorsement

4. The Home Day Care Endorsement does NOT cover

A. Liability
B. Medical payments
C. Corporal punishment
D. Premises business furnishings and equipment

5. The premium for the Home Day Care Endorsement is determined by

A. The age of the children
B. The experience of the provider
C. The square footage of the home
D. The number of children under care

6. The Homeowners forms do NOT cover earthquake without endorsement. However, the endorsement covers earthquakes, landslides, volcanic eruptions and earth movements that occur within what period of time as if they were a single loss?

A. 24 hours
B. 48 hours
C. 72 hours
D. 96 hours

7. The watercraft endorsement under Section II liability of the Homeowners Policy EXCLUDES

A. Any sailing vessel in excess of 26 feet
B. Water skiing, scuba or other equipment
C. Scheduled watercraft with inboard or inboard-outdrive power
D. Watercraft up to 26 feet long with outboard motors in excess of 25 HP

8. The business pursuits endorsement would NOT be available for

A. Sole proprietors
B. Office employees
C. Sales representatives
D. Public school teachers

9. The personal injury endorsement would NOT cover

A. False arrest
B. Libel and slander
C. Malicious prosecution
D. Damage to personal property

10. The limited fungi, wet or dry rot, or bacteria coverage EXCLUDES

A. Liability resulting from contact with mold
B. The cost to remove mold from covered property
C. Fungi that are part of a product intended for consumption
D. The cost to tear out and replace any part of the building to gain access to the mold

1-A   2-B   3-D   4-C   5-D   6-C   7-B   8-A   9-D   10-C

III. COMMERCIAL PACKAGE POLICY (CPP)

The Commercial Package Policy (effective December 1, 1995) includes both property insurance and general liability insurance. It is eligible to become a "package" policy, with a package policy discount.

Components of a commercial policy

Common policy declarations
First named insured. The party responsible for the payment of premiums, authorized to make changes in the policy terms, to cancel the policy and receive notice of cancellation.

Common policy conditions
Cancellation. 30 days advance notice to insured; 10 days advance notice for nonpayment of premium.

Policy conditions may be changed only by an endorsement issued by the insurer.

The insurer is granted the right to audit books and records of the insured relating to the policy for a period of up to THREE years after the end of the policy period.

The insurer is granted the right to make inspections, surveys, reports, and recommendations only with the written consent of the insured.

In the event of the insured's death, rights and duties are automatically transferred to the insured's legal representative or anyone having temporary custody of the property.

Interline endorsements are common to several coverage parts and are used **as needed.**

One or more coverage parts When a policy uses only one of the seven coverage parts, it is a monoline commercial policy. When it has more than one part, it is a package policy.

IV. COMMERCIAL PROPERTY

Commercial property conditions form
The insured is permitted to bring suit within 2 years of loss, instead of the 12 months required under the Standard Fire Policy. The policy territory includes the United States, Canada and Puerto Rico.

The commercial property **coverage forms** identify the property to be insured. Some are direct loss coverages while some are indirect or consequential loss coverages. We need to know these 8 forms:

> **Building and personal property**
> **Builders risk**
> **Business income**
> **Extra expense**
> **Legal liability**
> **Glass coverage**
> **Condominium association**
> **Condominium commercial unit-owners**

These property coverage forms must be used with one of 4 **"Causes of Loss Forms"** which specify the perils for which coverage is provided, along with the relevant exclusions.

Basic Form
1. Covers fire, lightning, *windstorm, hail, aircraft, riot, vehicles, explosion, smoke, *vandalism, *sprinkler leakage, sinkhole collapse and volcanic action.
*can be excluded by endorsement

2. Sonic boom is not excluded. Damage by owned vehicles is excluded. The cost of filling a sinkhole is not covered.

3. EXCLUSIONS: building ordinance, earth movement, governmental action, nuclear hazard, power failure, water and war

1. Under the common policy conditions of the commercial package policy, who is the party responsible for the payment of premiums?

A. Insured
B. Insurer
C. Named insured
D. First named insured

2. Notice of cancellation under the commercial package policy for nonpayment of premium is

A. 10 days
B. 15 days
C. 20 days
D. 30 days

3. Policy conditions may be changed only by

A. The insured
B. An insurance agent
C. An officer of the insurer
D. An endorsement issued by the insurer

4. The insurer is granted the right to audit books and records of the insured relating to the policy for a period of up to how many years after the end of the policy period?

A. 1 years
B. 2 years
C. 3 years
D. 4 years

5. The insurer is granted the right to make inspections, surveys, reports, and recommendations

A. Annually
B. At any time
C. Only at renewal
D. Only with the written consent of the insured

6. In the event of the insured's death, rights and duties are automatically transferred to the insured's

A. Spouse
B. Beneficiary
C. Power of Attorney
D. Legal representative

7. Under the commercial property conditions form, the insured is permitted to bring suit within how many years?

A. 12 months
B. 18 months
C. 24 months
D. 36 months

8. The policy territory of the commercial property form EXCLUDES

A. Canada
B. Mexico
C. Puerto Rico
D. United States

9. The Basic Cause of Loss Form may EXCLUDE which of the following by endorsement?

A. Fire
B. Smoke
C. Explosion
D. Sprinkler leakage

10. The Basic Cause of Loss Form covers

A. Sonic boom
B. Power failure
C. Earth movement
D. Governmental action

1-D 2-A 3-D 4-C 5-D   6-D 7-C 8-B 9-D 10-A

Broad Form
1. All of the basic form perils plus breakage of glass, ($100 per plate and $500 per occurrence), falling objects, weight of snow, ice or sleet, water damage.

2. Collapse coverage is included for these specific perils only; insured perils, hidden decay, hidden insect or vermin damage, weight of contents, equipment, animals, or people, weight of rain on a roof, and defects in materials or methods used in construction, only if the collapse occurs during the course of construction.

3. Collapse does not include settling, cracking, shrinkage, bulging, or expansion.

Special Form
1. Coverage is on an OPEN PERILS basis for risks of direct physical loss.

2. EXCLUSIONS INCLUDE: explosion of steam boilers, wear and tear, fungus, rust, decay, deterioration, animals, and (rain, snow, ice or sleet) to property in the open.

The **Earthquake Form** covers earthquake and volcanic eruption, explosion, or effusion during the policy period or within 168 hours after policy expiration. It excludes artificially generated electric current, fire, explosion, landslide and mudflow.

Selected endorsements
    Ordinance or law provides coverage for contingent liability due to building law enforcement.

    Peak season limit of insurance is used when the period of fluctuation is temporary, and the extent of the fluctuation is known.

    Spoilage coverage is for loss to perishable stock caused by power failure either on or off premises or for equipment or mechanical failure.

    Value reporting form is used for fluctuating business inventories.

BUILDINGS AND PERSONAL PROPERTY COVERAGE FORM
This is the standard form for insuring most types of business property for direct damage coverage on completed buildings and structures, contents, yard property and personal property of others. The form can be used to write coverage on buildings or contents or both.

The limits of insurance applies on a "per occurrence" basis which means that the amount of insurance is not reduced by loss.

The coverage is provided under **3 DEFINITIONS:**
1. Building
2. Your Business Personal Property
3. Personal Property of Others

There are **3 ADDITIONAL COVERAGES:**
Debris Removal, Preservation of Property, Fire Department Service Charges

There are **6 COVERAGE EXTENSIONS** which apply only when the policy is written with 80% or higher coinsurance.
1. Newly Acquired Buildings
2. Newly Acquired Personal Property
3. Personal Effects and Property of Others Coverage Extension
4. Valuable Papers and Records Extension
5. Property Off Premises Coverage Extension
6. Outdoor Property Coverage Extension

All of the coverage extension limits and the Fire Department Service Charge limit are additional amounts of insurance.

There are **3 OPTIONAL COVERAGES**
Agreed Value Optional Coverage suspends the coinsurance provisions, guaranteeing that the insured will not suffer a coinsurance penalty.

Inflation guard provides that the increase in the amount of insurance will occur steadily over the period of the year for which the coverage is provided.

Replacement Cost Coverage provides for payment on a replacement cost basis

1. The Broad cause of loss form covers collapse due to

A. Expansion
B. Falling objects
C. Settling and cracking
D. Shrinkage and bulging

2. Coverage under the Special cause of loss form is on the basis of

A. Open perils
B. Named perils
C. Specific perils
D. Comprehensive perils

3. The Earthquake Form covers earthquake and volcanic eruption, explosion, or effusion during the policy period or within how many hours after policy expiration?

A. 24 hours
B. 48 hours
C. 168 hours
D. 240 hours

4. The earthquake cause of loss form covers

A. Fire
B. Mudflow
C. Landslide
D. Volcanic eruption

5. Which of the following is NOT an optional coverage endorsement to the Building and Personal Property Form?

A. Ordinance or law
B. Spoilage coverage
C. Value reporting form
D. Builders risk coverage form

6. The form to be used for fluctuating business inventories is the

A. Blanket form
B. Earnings form
C. Inventory form
D. Value reporting form

7. The Building and Personal Property coverage form would NOT include

A. Completed additions
B. Fixtures, including outdoor fixtures
C. Bridges, walks, patios, and other paved surfaces
D. Outdoor furniture, floor coverings and certain appliances

8. All of the coverage extension limits and the Fire Department Service Charge limit are

A. Additional amounts of insurance
B. Available without regard to coinsurance percentages
C. Included in the limit of insurance for the buildings
D. Reductions in the amount of insurance

9. The optional coverage in the Buildings and Personal Property Coverage Form which suspends the coinsurance provisions, guaranteeing that the insured will not suffer a coinsurance penalty is

A. Agreed value
B. Inflation guard
C. Replacement cost
D. Value reporting form

10. Which optional coverage provides that the increase in the amount of insurance will occur steadily over the period of the year for which the coverage is provided?

A. Agreed value
B. Inflation guard
C. Replacement cost
D. Value reporting form

1-B   2-A   3-C   4-D   5-D   6-D   7-C   8-A   9-A   10-B

BUILDERS RISK COVERAGE FORM

Used when a building under construction is to be insured. "We will not pay a greater share of any loss than the proportion that the Limit of Insurance bears to the value on the date of completion of the building described in the Declarations."

(Insurance Limit)
---------------------- X Loss) - deductible = Payment
(Completed Value)

BUSINESS INCOME COVERAGE

1. Designed to indemnify business firms for expenses that continue and profits that would have been earned during the period required to restore property damaged by an insured peril to a useful condition.

2. The insured is required to use all reasonable means to resume operations as soon as possible.

3. "Business income" is the sum of net profit that would have been earned and necessary continuing expenses including payroll that are incurred during the "period of restoration" caused by direct loss at the described premises.

4. The coverage is written subject to a coinsurance provision.

EXTRA EXPENSE COVERAGE

It provides payment for expenses above normal costs when such expenses are incurred to continue operations after damage to the premises by an insured peril for those enterprises that can continue operations with other facilities. (service related businesses, banks, insurance agencies, accounting firms)

LEGAL LIABILITY (covered under the Commercial General Liability section)

GLASS COVERAGE FORM

The Glass Coverage Form may be combined with other Coverage Forms in the Commercial Property Coverage Part, or it may be written on its own. Coverage is on a broad open perils basis.

1. The insured is indemnified for accidental glass breakage (except by fire) and damage caused by acids or chemicals accidentally or maliciously applied.
2. The only exclusions are fire, war, and nuclear damage.
3. Only those plate glass panels specifically scheduled are insured.
4. Lettering and ornamentation are not covered unless they have been specifically insured.
5. The policy also covers the cost of repairing or replacing frames or sashes, boarding up or installing temporary plates in broken windows, and removing and replacing fixtures or other obstructions.

CONDOMINIUM ASSOCIATION

This commercial property form covers the buildings in a condominium complex, business personal property owned by the association or owned indivisibly by all unit-owners, and personal property of others in the care, custody or control of the association while it is located at the premises.

It does not cover personal property owned, used or controlled by a unit-owner. It excludes fixtures, improvements, alterations, and appliances which can be added by endorsement if the Association Agreement requires the association to insure the property.

CONDOMINIUM COMMERCIAL UNIT-OWNERS

This form covers the owner of a commercial condominium. It covers the unit-owner's business personal property and the personal property of others in the insured's care, custody or control. (i.e., contents, business personal property, and the personal property of others).

It does not cover buildings. It excludes fixtures, improvements, alterations, and appliances in units unless the Association Agreement places responsibility for insuring them on the unit-owner.

1. The Builders Risk Form coverage would cease in all of the following cases EXCEPT

A. Immediately after construction is completed
B. When the insured's interest in the property ceases
C. Whenever the property is accepted by the purchaser
D. 60 days after the constructed building is occupied or put into its intended use

2. The Builders Risk coverage form can be used to cover

A. Land or water
B. Farm buildings under construction
C. Lawns, trees, shrubs or plants when outside of buildings
D. Radio and television antennas when outside of buildings

3. Business income coverage forms pay for all of the following EXCEPT

A. Payroll
B. Net income
C. Accounts receivable
D. Necessary continuing expenses

4. Which commercial property form would cover the extra expenses needed to continue operations at any cost?

A. Loss of use coverage form
B. Extra expense coverage form
C. Business income coverage form
D. Operations expense coverage form

5. The Legal Liability coverage form covers damage to property of others while in the insured's control

A. Only while on premises
B. For a wide range of losses
C. Only while occupying another's building
D. Only if the insured is legally liable for the damage

6. The glass coverage form would NOT cover

A. Plate glass
B. Damage caused by acids
C. Accidental glass breakage
D. Malicious scratching of glass

7. The Condominium Form that provides coverage for the building is

A. Homeowners Form 6
B. Condominium unit owner's form
C. Condominium association form
D. Commercial building and personal property form

8. The Condominium form that covers business personal property owned by the condominium association is

A. Condominium association form
B. The Homeowners Form 6 Policy
C. Condominium commercial unit-owners form
D. Both the association form and the commercial unit-owners form

9. The Condominium Commercial Unit-Owners Form does NOT cover

A. Contents
B. Buildings
C. Personal property of others
D. Business personal property of the unit owner

10. The Condominium Commercial Unit-Owners Form provides coverage on fixtures, improvements, alterations and appliances

A. By endorsement
B. Automatically as part of the business personal property
C. When the condominium association form excludes them
D. Without payment of an additional premium

1-A   2-B   3-C   4-B   5-D   6-D   7-C   8-A   9-B   10-A

V. EQUIPMENT BREAKDOWN

Equipment breakdown covers boilers and any machine subject to accidental breakdown that could destroy or damage a large part of the machine. It has its own declarations page.

EXAMPLES motors, generators, transformers, switchboards, steam, oil and gas engines, flywheels, turbines, hydraulic presses, air compressors, and refrigeration equipment.

Much of the premium dollar goes for the inspection service which does not obligate the insurer to make inspections. However, all parties involved understand that the inspections will be made and coverage suspended until repairs are made.

Equipment breakdown protection coverage form (BM 00 20)

Breakdown is defined as a sudden and accidental equipment breakdown such as pressure or vacuum equipment, mechanical failure or electrical failure.

Covered Property includes: equipment, loss of property in your care, custody or control and for which you are legally liable, expediting expenses, business income and extra expense, spoilage damage, utility interruption, newly acquired premises, ordinance or law coverage, errors and omissions in describing the property to be insured, brands and labels, contingent business income and extra expense. Note: bodily injury liability is excluded.

Exclusions Damage due to testing of any object is specifically excluded, flood, earth movement, ordinance or law if not caused by breakdown, nuclear hazard war or military action, neglect by the insured, deterioration, corrosion, erosion, wear and tear (resulting damage is covered), fire or combustion explosion.

Limitations A maximum of $25,000 will be paid for ammonia contamination, consequential loss, data and media, hazardous substance, and water damage unless a higher limit is shown in the declarations.

Valuation. The valuation condition provides that payment for loss will be made on a replacement cost basis if the insured repairs or replaces the property within 24 months. Subsequent settlement is limited to the smaller of ACV or cost to repair or replace.

An additional 25% will be paid if the repair improves the environment, increases efficiency or enhances safety.

Suspension If the insurer discovers during an inspection that covered equipment is exposed to a dangerous condition, coverage may be suspended immediately. It can be reinstated by endorsement after compliance with the insurer's recommendations.

Deductibles A separate deductible applies for each applicable coverage unless the deductible is a combined deductible. If more than one covered equipment is damaged, only the highest deductible applies.

Selected endorsements

Actual cash value (BM 99 59)

Business income – Report of values (BM 15 31)

The insured reports net sales, commissions, and expenses to the insurer within three months of the report date indicated in the Declarations and every anniversary thereafter to determine the premium charge for business interruption coverage. Noncompliance results in a 100% coinsurance requirement.

1. The equipment breakdown coverage part of the Commercial Package Policy

A. Has its own declarations page
B. Covers bodily injury to employees
C. Does not provide an inspection service
D. Covers property damage and bodily injury

2. Equipment breakdown covers

A. Bodily injury
B. Expediting expenses
C. Neglect by the insured
D. Flood and earth movement

3. Equipment breakdown coverage EXCLUDES

A. Electrical objects
B. Direct damage to covered property
C. Damage due to testing of any object
D. Loss to property in the insured's care, custody and control

4. All of the following are coverage's under the equipment breakdown protection form EXCEPT

A. Spoilage damage
B. Brands and labels
C. Utility interruption
D. Fire or combustion explosion

5. Equipment breakdown does NOT cover

A. Electrical failure
B. Mechanical failure
C. Failure of vacuum equipment
D. Viruses in computer programs

6. The valuation condition provides that payment for loss will be made on a replacement cost basis if the insured repairs or replaces the property within how many months?

A. 12 months
B. 18 months
C. 24 months
D. 36 months

7. If a repair improves the environment, increases efficiency or enhances safety, what additional percent will be paid?

A. 10%
B. 25%
C. 30%
D. 45%

8. The insured reports net sales, commissions, and expenses to the insurer within three months of the report date indicated in the Declarations and every anniversary thereafter to determine the premium charge for business interruption coverage. Noncompliance results in

A. Nonrenewal of coverage
B. Cancellation of coverage
C. An 80% coinsurance requirement
D. A 100% coinsurance requirement

1-A   2-B   3-C   4-D   5-D   6-C   7-B   8-D

VI. INLAND MARINE

Transportation or "marine" insurance is for property that is primarily mobile in nature.

The **"Nationwide Marine Definition"** establishes the types of property covered under marine insurance, both inland and ocean. It lists the categories of property that marine insurers are allowed to insure. The 6 covered categories are: Imports, Exports, Domestic shipments, Bridges & tunnels, Personal property floater risks, and Commercial property floater risks.

Personal Articles Floaters provide scheduled coverage for nine optional classes of personal property wherever it is located such as jewelry, furs, cameras, musical instruments, silverware, golf equipment, fine arts, stamps and coins.

Commercial inland marine conditions form. Valuation is the lesser of actual cash value or replacement value.

Inland marine coverage forms

Accounts Receivable covers sums of money due the insured from customers which became uncollectible due to loss, damage to or destruction of accounts receivable records.

Bailees Customer Bailee coverage insures against loss of property belonging to others and entrusted to the bailee. The Bailee Customer's Policy covers fire, lightning, perils of transportation, burglary, holdup but not wear and tear.

Commercial articles. Cameras, musical instruments and related equipment

Contractors Equipment Floater Coverage on equipment used by contractors in road building, construction, mining, such as power shovels, tractors, bulldozers, concrete mixers and hand tools written on a scheduled basis or blanket basis.

Electronic Data Processing equipment, data processing media, extra expenses and business interruption incurred in the loss of media.

Equipment Dealers stock in trade, such as construction, agricultural and other mobile equipment.

Installation Floater Turbines, transformers and air conditioning equipment during transit or installation.

Jewelers Block Covers owned stock, property of customers in the insured's custody and property of other jewelers in the insured's custody, but excludes property exhibited in showcases or windows away from the described premises. It covers watches worn solely for purposes of adjustment but excludes other property while being worn by the insured, an employee, or a family member of either.

Signs including automatic and/or neon types.

Valuable Papers and Records May be written to insure various types of important records, including maps, film, tape, wire or recording media, drawings, abstracts, deeds, mortgages, and manuscripts.

1. Which of the following types of property is not a category under the Nationwide Marine Definition?

A. Imports
B. Exports
C. Warehouses
D. Bridges and tunnels

2. The commercial inland marine conditions form states that valuation is the lesser of

A. Agreed value or replacement cost
B. Actual cash value or market value
C. Historical cost or replacement cost
D. Actual cash value or replacement value

3. The accounts receivable form excludes

A. Accounting errors
B. Loss of accounts receivable records
C. Damage to accounts receivable records
D. Collection expenses above normal amounts

4. The Inland Marine form that covers a customer's property while in the insured business's control for cleaning, repairing or servicing is

A. Floor plan
B. Installation
C. Bailees customer
D. Commercial articles

5. The one who owns the property held by someone else for some special purpose and then returned to the owner is the

A. Bailee
B. Bailor
C. Insured
D. Bailment

6. A John Deere implement dealer would use which inland marine form to cover stock in trade

A. Equipment dealers
B. Installation floater
C. Commercial articles
D. Contractors equipment floater

7. The Jewelers Block coverage form covers

A. Jewelry that is sold but not delivered
B. Unexplained disappearance of jewelry
C. Jewelry at an exhibition promoted by a trade association
D. Jewelry exhibited in showcases or show windows away from the premises

1-C   2-D   3-A   4-C   5-B   6-A   7-A

Transportation Coverages

Common carrier cargo liability is for carriers who offer their services to the public at large.

Legal liability for damage to property they are transporting is born by a common carrier.

Straight Bill of Lading is a document issued by a common carrier evidencing receipt of goods for shipment.

Released Bill of Lading limits the common carrier liability to a specified maximum dollar amount.

Contract carriers offer their services only to specific clients and are only liable when they are negligent.

Mail Form (Registered Mail Policy) Written for banks, trust companies, insurance companies, and similar firms that have occasion to mail money or other items of high value. It covers first class mail.

Motor truck cargo forms

Truckers form A liability coverage designed to indemnify public truckers against their legal liability for loss or damage to merchandise in their possession.

Shippers form Designed to provide transportation coverage for the owner of the goods for loss to those goods that have been shipped by a trucker operating as a common carrier or contract carrier.

Owners form Designed to provide transportation coverage for the business firms' own goods which it transports on its' own trucks.

Transit coverage forms Protects property of all kinds being shipped to others or being received.

Annual form Covers incoming and outgoing goods on an annual basis.

Trip form covers goods that are shipped for one specific trip.

VII. OCEAN MARINE

Major coverages on either an All Risk or Named Peril basis include: **Hull Insurance, Cargo Insurance, Freight Insurance, Protection and Indemnity (liability).**

Valuation Clause Almost all ocean marine policies are valued contracts and are written on a valued basis.

Implied warranties contained in ocean marine insurance require the vessel and its cargo to be (1) seaworthy (competent captain and crew), (2) legal (the venture is of legal purpose), (3) the cargo to be properly packaged (condition of cargo), and (4) the vessel must not deviate in its voyage.

Perils of the sea include wind, wave action, collision, stranding, sinking or capsizing.

Perils on the sea include fire, lightning, earthquake, pirates and thieves, jettison, barratry or fraud and all other like perils, losses and misfortune.

Loss adjustment by **General Average** means that any partial loss resulting from a deliberate and voluntary sacrifice for the benefit of all concerned, will be shared in proportion to their interest.

Loss adjustment by **Particular Average** has no requirement to share the loss when there is a partial loss.

49

1. The carrier who offers services to the public at large rather than to specific clients is a

A. Contract carrier
B. Common carrier
C. Motor truck carrier
D. Transportation carrier

2. The document issued by a common carrier evidencing receipt of goods for shipment and limits the common carrier liability to a specified maximum dollar amount is the

A. Mail form
B. Truckers form
C. Straight bill of lading
D. Released bill of lading

3. A carrier who only offers its services to specific clients and is only liable when negligent is a

A. Contract carrier
B. Common carrier
C. Motor truck carrier
D. Transportation carrier

4. The registered mail policy does NOT cover

A. Jewelry
B. First class mail
D. Stock certificates
C. Travelers checks

5. The transportation coverage that covers goods that are shipped for one specific trip is the

A. Owners form
B. Shippers form
C. Trip transit form
D. Annual transit form

6. Ocean marine legal liability is covered by

A. Cargo coverage
B. Loss adjustment
C. Implied warranties
D. Protection and Indemnity

7. The implied warranties of ocean marine insurance does NOT require

A. The vessel to be seaworthy
B. The vessel to deviate in its voyage
C. The venture to be of legal purpose
D. The cargo to be properly packaged

8. Perils of the sea include

A. Fire
B. Wind
C. Lightning
D. Earthquake

9. Perils on the sea include

A. Sinking
B. Jettison
C. Stranding
D. Capsizing

10. Under ocean marine insurance, in the event of a partial loss in which there is no requirement to share the loss, loss adjustment is by

A. Mean average
B. Rolling average
C. General average
D. Particular average

1-B   2-D   3-A   4-A   5-C   6-D   7-B   8-B   9-B   10-D

50

VIII. NATIONAL FLOOD INSURANCE PROGRAM

Since 1983, the program has been conducted as a partnership between the federal government and the private insurance industry, under what is known as the **"Write-Your-Own"** program.

Flood insurance policies are issued both by the **government** and by the over 300 private insurers participating in the program, who issue policies in their own names.

Eligibility. The HUD Act of 1968 established a federally subsidized flood insurance program, under which flood insurance is made available to both individuals and to business firms.

There is a 30 waiting period for new applications or to increase coverage, with an exception for a requirement to procure flood insurance to satisfy a home loan.

Coverage. Flood is defined in the policy as a general and temporary condition of partial or complete inundation of normally dry land areas, resulting from overflow of inland or tidal waters or the unusual and rapid accumulation or runoff of surface waters from any source. The flood must be on 2 or more properties or 1 property plus 2 acres.

Coverage is also provided against loss by mud slides which are caused or precipitated by accumulation of water on or under the ground. It does not cover rain, sleet, snow or sewer backup into a dwelling.

Limits. For a single-family dwelling under the emergency plan, coverage is available at subsidized rates for up to $35,000 on the dwelling and $10,000 on the contents.

Under the regular plan, coverage is up to $250,000 on the dwelling and $100,000 on contents.

Nonresidential and Small Business coverage is available on building/contents for $100,000/$100,000 under the NFIP Emergency Program and $500,000/$500,000 under the Regular Program.

Deductible. The $500 deductible applies separately to the dwelling and the contents under the regular plan. Under the emergency plan, the deductible is $1000.

IX. OTHER PROPERTY COVERAGES

1. Earthquake coverage can be by endorsement or as a separate policy for damage to a structure, its contents or both. Multiple shocks within a 72 hour period are treated as a single earthquake.

The Earthquake Form covers earthquake and volcanic eruption. It excludes artificially generated electric current, fire, explosion, landslide and mudflow.

2. Mobile Homes can be covered by a separate mobile home policy, the dwelling basic form, or by endorsement to the HO 2 or HO 3. The mobile home must be used for year round living, and must be at least 10 feet wide and 40 feet long.

3. Personal Watercraft
The **Boatowners/watercraft package policy** provides open-peril coverage for property, liability, and medical payments on an actual cash value basis for watercraft under a specific length and dollar value.

Personal Yacht Policies for larger boats provide open peril property and liability coverage on the hull, boat trailer, protection and indemnity (liability), and medical payments.

4. Crop/hail insurance covers hail, fire and lightning on growing crops.

5. Windstorm covers damage from wind.

1. The waiting period for new applications or to increase coverage under the National Flood Insurance Program is

A. 15 days
B. 30 days
C. 45 days
D. 60 days

2. A flood would NOT be covered if it was on

A. Two or more properties
B. One property plus 2 acres
C. Property lost due to mudslides
D. Property flooded by sewer backup

3. The Flood Policy excludes the peril of

A. Rain
B. Runoff
C. Mudslide
D. Surface water

4. The Flood Policy covers

A. Septic tanks
B. Fog and mist
C. Retaining walls
D. Mudslides and mudflows

5. The total amount of insurance available for the dwelling of a single family residence under the Regular Program of the National Flood Insurance Program is:

A. $35,000
B. $100,000
C. $250,000
D. $500,000

6. Under the National Flood Insurance Regular Program for nonresidential and small businesses, the maximum coverage available for the buildings is

A. $250,000
B. $500,000
C. $750,000
D. $1,000,000

7. The earthquake form covers earthquake and

A. Fire
C. Landslide
B. Mudflow
D. Volcanic eruption

8. Coverage for a mobile home does NOT require the mobile home to be

A. At least 10 years old
B. At least 10 feet wide
C. At least 40 feet long
D. Used for year round living

9. The Boatowners Property Coverage would cover

A. Portable televisions
B. Parasails and hang gliders
C. Anchors, oars and life preservers
D. Hunting, fishing or other sporting equipment

10. The crop hail policy does NOT cover

A. Hail
B. Fire
C. Lightning
D. Windstorm

1-B   2-D   3-A   4-D   5-C   6-B   7-D   8-B   9-C   10-D

X. BUSINESSOWNERS ('02) POLICY (BOP)

Characteristics and purpose
The BOP is written on a Special Form (open perils) basis for replacement cost. It is designed for smaller firms and medium sized apartments, offices, mercantile, service or processing occupancies, some contractors, small fast food restaurants, convenience stores with gasoline pumps and limited laundries and dry cleaners. It excludes automobile type businesses.

Businessowners Section I – Property
Definitions Coverage Territory means the United States, its territories and possessions, Puerto Rico and Canada.

Coverage on both buildings and contents is for replacement cost and there is no coinsurance provision.

Business interruption and extra expense are automatically included. There is no limit of liability and no coinsurance clause, and the insured may collect for reduced earnings for up to 12 months.

Business personal property off premises and in transit is covered up to $1,000.

Causes of loss The BOP Special Form provides coverage for risks of direct and indirect physical loss.

The Named Perils Endorsement can be added to provide named peril coverage for windstorm, civil commotion, smoke, hail, aircraft, vehicles, explosion, riot, fire, lightning, vandalism, sprinkler leakage, sinkhole collapse, volcanic action, and transportation damage to property in transit.

Exclusions include ordinance or law, earth movement, governmental action, nuclear hazard, power failure off premises, war, military action, water, and computer failure or malfunctioning.

Conditions The insurer may cancel the policy if the covered building has been vacant or unoccupied for 60 or more consecutive days.

Limits of insurance are indicated in the declarations.

Deductibles Standard deductible is $500.

Optional coverages include outdoor signs, money & securities for theft, employee dishonesty, and mechanical breakdown.

Businessowners Section II - Liability

Business liability The BOP ('02) Liability Coverage Form covers bodily injury, property damage, and advertising injury liability. It covers personal injury arising out of false arrest, detention or imprisonment. It does NOT cover employer's liability.

Bodily injury resulting from use of reasonable force to protect persons or property is covered.

Medical expenses Under the medical expense coverage, expenses must be incurred and reported within one year of the date of the accident. The injury does NOT have to be the result of the insureds' negligence to be covered.

Covered expenses include funeral services, first aid treatment at the time of the accident, and injury caused by the insureds operations.

Limits on basic business liability is $300,000, medical payments $5,000 and fire legal liability is $50,000.

Conditions regarding bankruptcy, duties in the event of occurrence, claim or suit, financial responsibility laws, legal action against us and separation of insureds.

Exclusions are similar to the commercial general liability coverage part.

Businessowners Section III – Common Policy Conditions

The conditions specify that if other insurance covers the same loss, the BOP will pay the excess over the other insurance.

1. Eligible risks under the Businessowners Policy would include

A. Bars
B. Banks
C. Carpenters
D. Auto dealers

2. The Businessowners Policy could NOT be written to cover

A. Funeral homes
B. Coin distributors
C. Plumbing contractors
D. Banks and credit unions

3. The named perils endorsement of the Businessowners Policy covers

A. Explosion
B. Power failure
C. Earth movement
D. Mechanical breakdown

4. Which of the following is NOT an additional coverage under the the Businessowners Policy?

A. Civil authority
B. Sinkhole collapse
C. Seepage of ground water
D. Pollutant cleanup and removal

5. The Businessowners Policy excludes

A. Extra expense
B. Wear and tear
C. Business income
D. Collapse caused by a specified peril

6. Under the Businessowners Policy Common Policy Conditions, the insurer may cancel for vacancy or unoccupancy of

A. 30 days or more
B. 60 days or more
C. 90 days or more
D. 120 days or more

7. The Businessowners Liability coverage covers

A. Bodily injury and property damage only
B. Bodily injury, property damage, and personal injury
C. Bodily injury, property damage and workers compensation
D. Bodily injury, property damage, advertising liability and personal injury

8. The Businessowners Liability Coverage excludes damages arising from

A. Product recall
B. Personal injury
C. Advertising injury
D. Medical expenses

9. The Businessowners Liability coverage covers

A. False arrest
B. Product recall
C. Liquor liability
D. Release of pollutants

10. The Businessowners Liability coverage excludes

A. Nonowned watercraft under 26 feet in length
B. Delays or failures to properly perform contracts
C. The operation of cherry pickers or similar devices
D. Watercraft on shore and on the insured's premises

1-C   2-D   3-A   4-C   5-B   6-B   7-D   8-A   9-A   10-B

XI. IOWA LAWS, RULES AND REGULATIONS PERTINENT TO PROPERTY INSURANCE ONLY

A. Iowa Basic Property Underwriting Association (FAIR PLAN)

Fair Access to Insurance Requirements (FAIR) Plans are designed to provide insurance to property owners in inner city and other high risk areas who are unable to obtain insurance through normal market channels because of the location of their property or other factors over which they have no control.

The FAIR plan provides property coverages, and extended coverages (EC), but excludes flood, earthquake and mine subsidence.

The reinsurance program, for which private insurers pay a premium, protects the private insurers against catastrophic losses from civil disorders.

Participation in the reinsurance program is optional on a state-by-state basis.

B. Cancellation/Nonrenewal
Forfeiture of policies--notice.

A policy or contract of insurance shall not be forfeited, suspended, or canceled except by notice to the insured.

A **notice of cancellation** is not effective unless mailed or delivered by the insurer to the named insured at least **20 days** before the effective date of cancellation.

Where cancellation is for **nonpayment of a premium** at least **10 days** prior to the date of cancellation.

The notice and reason for cancellation or nonrenewal may be made in person, or by sending by mail a letter addressed to the insured at the insured's address as given in or upon the policy.

An insurer shall not fail to **renew a policy** except by notice to the insured.

A **notice of intention not to renew** is not effective unless mailed or delivered by the insurer to the named insured **at least 30 days prior** to the expiration date of the policy and **at least 45 days prior** to the expiration date of a **commercial** insurance policy.

The insurer must give **45 days** notice to the insured for an increase of 25% on a renewal premium or deductible.

Cancellation of policy--notice to insured or mortgagee.

If the policy is **canceled by the insured**, the insured may pay to the company the customary **short rates** and costs of action.

If the policy is **canceled by the insurance company**, the insurer may retain only the **pro rata premium**.

If the initial cash premium, or any part of the premium, has not been paid, the policy may be canceled by the insurance company by giving notice to the insured and **ten days' notice to the mortgagee**, or other person to whom the policy is made payable, if any.

Policy restored.

At any time before cancellation of the policy for nonpayment of any premium, the insured may pay to the insurer the full amount due, including court costs if any, and from the date of such payment, or the collection of the judgment, the policy shall revive and be in full force and effect, provided such payment is made during the term of the policy and before a loss occurs.

Right of insured to cancel.

No provision, stipulation, or agreement to the contrary shall avoid or defeat the right of any insured to have the policy canceled.

1. The FAIR Plan makes insurance available to risks that were previously considered uninsurable because of

A. Moral risks
B. Morale risks
C. Physical risks
D. Environmental risks

2. The FAIR plan covers

A. Flood
B. Property
C. Earthquake
D. Mine subsidence

3. Which of the following exposures is insurable under the FAIR Plan?

A. Property subject to poor housekeeping
B. Property in violation of building codes
C. Property in violation of law or public policy
D. Property subject to environmental hazards beyond the control of the insured

4. A notice of cancellation is not effective unless mailed or delivered by the insurer to the named insured at least

A. 7 days before the effective date of cancellation
B. 10 days before the effective date of cancellation
C. 20 days before the effective date of cancellation
D. 30 days before the effective date of cancellation

5. A notice of cancellation for nonpayment of premium shall not be effective unless mailed or delivered by the insurer to the named insured at least

A. 10 days prior to the date of cancellation
B. 15 days prior to the date of cancellation
C. 20 days prior to the date of cancellation
D. 30 days prior to the date of cancellation

6. A notice of intention not to renew a commercial insurance policy is not effective unless mailed or delivered by the insurer to the named insured at least how many days prior to the expiration date of the policy?

A. 10 days
B. 20 days
C. 30 days
D. 45 days

7. For an increase of 25% on a renewal premium or deductible, the insurer must give how many days notice to the insured?

A. 10 days
B. 20 days
C. 30 days
D. 45 days

8. When the insurance company cancels an insurance policy, the return premium is

A. A flat cancellation
B. On a pro rata basis
C. On a short rate basis
D. A full premium refund

9. When an insured requests cancellation, the return premium is usually

A. A flat cancellation
B. On a pro rata basis
C. On a short rate basis
D. A full premium refund

10. If the initial cash premium, or any part of the premium, has not been paid, the policy may be canceled by the insurance company by giving notice of how many days to the mortgagee?

A. 10 days
B. 15 days
C. 20 days
D. 30 days

1-C   2-B   3-D   4-C   5-A   6-D   7-D   8-B   9-C   10-A

C. Standard Fire Policy

The Standard Fire Policy insures against direct loss by fire, lightning and by removal from premises endangered by the perils insured. It pays actual cash value.

When the Extended Coverage (EC) Endorsement is added to the Standard Fire Policy, the resulting policy is the Dwelling Basic Form (DP-1).

Uninsurable and excepted property. This policy shall not cover accounts, bills, currency, deeds, evidences of debt, money or securities; nor, unless specifically named hereon in writing, bullion or manuscripts.

Perils not included. This company shall not be liable for loss by fire or other perils insured against in this policy caused, directly or indirectly, by: *(a)* Enemy attack by armed forces, including action taken by military, naval or air forces in resisting an actual or an immediately impending enemy attack; *(b)* invasion; *(c)* insurrection; *(d)* rebellion; *(e)* revolution; *(f)* civil war; *(g)* usurped power; *(h)* order of any civil authority except acts of destruction at the time of and for the purpose of preventing the spread of fire, provided that such fire did not originate from any of the perils excluded by this policy; *(i)* neglect of the insured to use all reasonable means to save and preserve the property at and after a loss, or when the property is endangered by fire in neighboring premises; *(j)* nor shall this company be liable for loss by theft.

1. The Standard Fire Policy would NOT insure against direct loss by

A. Fire
B. Wind
C. Removal
D. Lightning

2. The Standard Fire Policy insures against direct loss by

A. Theft
B. Civil war
C. Lightning
D. Enemy attack

3. The Standard Fire Policy pays for losses on the basis of

A. Stated value
B. Fair market value
C. Replacement cost
D. Actual cash value

4. When the Extended Coverage (EC) Endorsement is added to the Standard Fire Policy, the resulting policy is the

A. Tenants Form
B. Dwelling Basic Form (DP-1)
C. Homeowners Broad Form (HO-2)
D. Homeowners Special Form (HO-3)

5. If specifically named in writing, the Standard Fire Policy shall cover

A. Deeds
B. Currency
C. Money or securities
D. Bullion or manuscripts

1-B   2-C   3-D   4-B   5-D

CASUALTY INSURANCE
TYPES OF CASUALTY POLICIES

I. PERSONAL AUTO POLICY
The Personal Auto Policy is divided into 6 parts.

Part A - Liability Coverage

(1) Bodily injury and property damage The liability insuring agreement obligates the insurer to pay, up to the policy limit, bodily injury and property damages for which any "Insured" becomes legally responsible because of an accident.

Any person using the covered auto with permission is covered for liability, but the State of Iowa holds the auto owner liable for damage caused by another person operating the auto with permission.

If a trailer and an automobile are being used together, liability coverage is automatically extended to the trailer. It provides liability coverage for the employer of the named insured if the employer should be sued because of the operation of an insured automobile by the named insured.

It covers damage caused by the insured to a private garage used by insured.

(2) Supplementary payments The premium on a bail bond with a maximum of $250, Premium on an appeal bond, Interest that accrues after a judgment is entered in any suit defended by the insurer, Loss of earnings up to $200/day for attendance at hearings/trials at company's request, and Reasonable expenses incurred at insurer's request.

(3) Exclusions The overall purpose of exclusions in an auto policy is to limit the coverages to purposes and rates for which the policy is written.

The liability coverage of the Personal Auto Policy excludes damage to property owned by the insured, the operation of the automobile as a public or livery conveyance (carrying persons for a fee), the operation by a covered person of a motorcycle, intentional acts causing bodily injury or property damage, and damage caused by insured to property being transported.

Part B - Medical Payments Coverage

It pays the necessary medical expenses incurred as a result of the use of a covered auto for the named insured, spouse and passengers.

Medical payments coverage includes surgical expense, dental expense, funeral expense, but not counseling expense.

NAMED INSURED AND FAMILY MEMBERS are covered for bodily injury caused by an accident while occupying a covered auto OR if they are struck by a vehicle designed for use on public roads or by a trailer of any type.

The medical payments coverage applies to the insured and family members if injured by someone else's motorcycle or car while walking as a pedestrian.

PERSONS OTHER THAN the named insured and family members are covered for medical payments only while occupying the insured's covered auto.

Part C – Uninsured Motorists Coverage

Uninsured motorists applies only when the other driver does not carry insurance, is a hit-and-run driver, or is insured by an insurer that becomes insolvent.

Uninsured Motorist Coverage protects against an uninsured motorist for bodily injury only.

Underinsured motorists applies when the other driver has insurance, but the limits of coverage are less than the amount to which the injured party would be entitled based on his/her injuries.

1. The Personal Auto Policy liability coverage covers

A. Property damage only
B. Bodily injury and property damage
C. Bodily injury, property damage, and personal injury
D. Bodily injury, property damage, personal injury, and advertising liability

2. Supplementary payments under the Personal Auto Policy do NOT cover

A. Carrying persons or property for a fee
B. Up to $200 per day for loss of earnings
C. Up to $250 toward the cost of bail bonds
D. Premiums on appeal or attachment bonds

3. The liability section of the Personal Auto Policy covers

A. A share-the-expense carpool
B. Operation of a vehicle used as a taxi
C. Bodily injury to an insured's employees
D. Bodily injury caused intentionally by the insured

4. Under the Personal Auto Policy, "Your covered auto" would NOT cover

A. Boat trailer
B. Utility trailer
C. A pickup truck used for delivery
D. A "loaner vehicle" used while the insured's auto is being repaired

5. Part A – Liability Coverage of the Personal Auto Policy would NOT provide coverage for

A. Defense costs
B. Interest charges levied on a verdict
C. Bodily injury and property damage
D. Damage to property owned or being transported by the insured

6. Medical payments under the Personal Auto Policy would cover

A. Vehicle used as a residence
B. Vehicle with less than four wheels
C. Funeral expenses resulting from accidental bodily injury
D. A person being struck by a vehicle in the course of work

7. Medical payments coverage of the Personal Auto Policy does NOT cover

A. The named insured and any family member
B. Reasonable medical expenses for necessary medical and funeral services
C. Injuries sustained while occupying a vehicle located for use as a residence or premises
D. Any person other than the insured while occupying the named insured's covered auto

8. Part C – Uninsured Motorists Coverage does NOT provide coverage for

A. An accident caused by a hit and run driver
B. An operator of a vehicle that is financially irresponsible
C. An operator of a vehicle whose insurance company becomes insolvent
D. Any vehicle owned by or furnished for the regular use of family members

9. Uninsured motorist pays benefits only for

A. Collision
B. Bodily injury
C. Comprehensive
D. Property damage

10. Which motorist coverage applies when the other driver has insurance, but does not have enough insurance to cover the amount due the injured party?

A. Uninsured motorist
B. Underinsured motorist
C. Comprehensive coverage
D. Bodily injury and property damage

1-B   2-A   3-A   4-C   5-D   6-C   7-C   8-D   9-B   10-B

Part D - Coverage for Damage to Your Auto

Physical damage includes collision; other than collision; specified perils. There is a single physical damage insuring agreement, which provides coverage on an open-perils basis.

Automobile Collision (physical damage) insurance under the PAP provides payment for losses to your car regardless of liability and is applicable whether the damage was due to your (the insured's) negligence or not.

Collision "The upset, or collision with another object of your covered auto."

Other than collision The perils specifically excluded from the definition of collision, which therefore make them "comprehensive" coverages are:

breakage of glass, loss caused by missiles, falling objects, fire, theft or larceny, explosion, earthquake, windstorm, hail, water, flood, malicious mischief or vandalism, riot or civil commotion, contact or collision with a bird or animal.

A major exclusion under the comprehensive coverage is loss due to collision.

Deductibles The deductible for collision and OTC are specified separately and they lower premiums. The deductible under the collision coverage is normally higher than that for other losses.

Part E covers Duties After an Accident or Loss

Part F is General Provisions.
The policy territory includes the United States, its territories and possessions, Puerto Rico, and Canada.

Who is an insured?

Auto must be owned by an individual OR by a husband and wife who are residents of the same household.

The named insured and any resident family member are covered for the use of any automobile.

Other persons are insured while using the covered automobile subject to the requirement that the use be with the reasonable belief that the person has a right to do so.

Types of Auto

Use and Eligibility of Auto Private passenger automobiles (includes pick-up trucks, vans, panel trucks, trailer owned by insured, auto leased by insured for a least 6 months), motorcycles, motor homes, golf carts, snowmobiles. It may not be used to carry property or persons for a fee or rented to others or used as a taxicab.

a. Owned auto - any private passenger auto, pickup truck, trailer, or van owned by or available for the regular use of the named insured or family member.

b. Non-owned auto – any private passenger auto, pickup truck, trailer, or van not owned by or available for the regular use of the named insured or a family member, e.g., a short-term rental car.

c. Hired auto – autos the insured leases, hires or borrows, but not from members of the insured's household.

d. Temporary Substitute auto, e.g., short-term rental car, is considered a non-owned auto instead of a covered auto under Physical Damage Coverage only.

e. Newly Acquired Autos – any private passenger auto or pickup or van that you become the owner of during the policy period.

1. In the Personal Auto Policy, collision is defined to cover

A. Flood
B. Breakage of glass
C. Upset of a vehicle
D. Contact with a bird or animal

2. Under Part D – Damage to Your Auto, all of the following losses are examples of Other Than Collision EXCEPT

A. Riot or civil commotion
B. Missiles or falling objects
C. Contact with a bird or animal
D. Overturning of the auto while driving too fast for conditions

3. Other Than Collision or Comprehensive coverage under the Personal Auto Policy EXCLUDES

A. Theft or larceny
B. Riot or civil commotion
C. Missiles or falling objects
D. Personal property in the vehicle

4. Which of the following is covered under the Personal Auto Physical Damage coverage?

A. CD players
B. Personal computers
C. Permanently installed telephones
D. Radar or laser detection equipment

5. Personal Auto Physical Damage coverage covers

A. Mechanical or electrical breakdown
B. Custom furnishings or equipment in a pickup or van
C. Any auto being used in a prearranged racing or speed contest
D. Sound equipment and its accessories that are permanently installed in the auto

6. The policy territory of the Personal Auto Policy does NOT include

A. Mexico
B. Canada
C. Puerto Rico
D. Territories and possessions of the U.S.

7. The auto policy would NOT cover

A. An individual
B. A husband and wife
C. A resident family member
D. A separated spouse after 90 days

8. Which of the following is NOT an insured under the auto policy of the auto owner?

A. A neighbor driving his own car
B. A neighbor driving the named insured's car
C. The son of the named insured driving a neighbor's car
D. Any person driving the named insured's covered auto with the reasonable belief that he is entitled to do so

9. A type of auto that would NOT be eligible for the personal auto policy would be

A. A motor home
B. An auto used as a taxicab
C. A pick-up truck, van or panel truck
D. An auto used to car pool children to a soccer game

10. A short-term rental car would be an example of a

A. Hired auto
B. Owned auto
C. Non-owned auto
D. Newly acquired auto

1-B   2-D   3-D   4-C   5-D   6-A   7-D   8-A   9-B   10-C

Transportation Expense and
Rental Reimbursement Expense

Covers a maximum amount per day ($20) for a
period beginning 48 hours after the theft and ending
when the auto is returned or the company pays for
the loss. There is a 24 hour waiting period for other
types of losses. Maximum $600.

Exclusions

The personal auto policy does not cover damage
caused intentionally by the insured, wear and tear,
freezing, and mechanical breakdown.

The auto policy covers damage to a non-owned auto
driven by the named insured, damages the insured is
entitled to collect from uninsured motorist, bodily
injury and property damages for which the insured is
liable, but not personal effects.

B. Personal Liability

Personal liability supplement
This endorsement providing Liability and Medical
payments may be added to an auto policy. It
provides coverage in the event a claim or suit is
brought against an insured by a third party for
damages because of bodily injury or property
damage caused by an occurrence.

63

1. Under the Personal Auto Policy the transportation expense coverage would NOT have a

A. Deductible
B. Waiting period
C. Maximum total limit
D. Maximum daily limit

2. Under a Personal Auto Policy, how much would be paid under transportation expense for a stolen auto after 5 days?

A. $40
B. $60
C. $80
D. $100

3. Under a Personal Auto Policy, how much would be paid under transportation expense for a damaged auto after 5 days?

A. $40
B. $60
C. $80
D. $100

4. The personal auto policy covers

A. Wear and tear
B. Personal effects of the insured
C. Freezing and mechanical breakdown
D. Bodily injury and property damage for which the insured is liable

5. The Personal Liability Supplement EXCLUDES

A. Legal defense
B. Expected or intended injury by the insured
C. Related interest charges levied on a verdict
D. Payment up to the limit of liability for damages for which the insured is legally liable

1-A   2-B   3-C   4-D   5-B

II. BUSINESS (COMMERCIAL) AUTO POLICY

The commercial auto policy has a declarations page, five different coverage forms to choose from, and a group of endorsements which may be added. The five commercial auto coverage forms are: Business Auto, Business Auto Physical Damage, Garage, Truckers, and Motor Carrier.

BUSINESS AUTO COVERAGE FORM

Section I – Covered Autos include passenger automobiles, buses, trucks and trailers. Covered classes include owned, leased, hired or borrowed business autos.

It does not include mobile equipment such as construction equipment, vehicles that are not required to be licensed, and vehicles designed for use principally off public roads.

Section II – Liability Coverage covers bodily injury, property damage and legal defense costs. Liability coverage includes mobile equipment while being carried or towed by a covered auto, temporary substitute autos, and trailers.

Uninsured motorist pays for bodily injury caused by a negligent motorist with no insurance.

Underinsured motorist pays for bodily injury caused by a negligent motorist with policy limits that are too low to pay for all the bodily injuries.

Liability Exclusions include contractual liability, workers compensation, indemnification for injury to employees, injury to fellow employees, injury to employees of the insured, care, custody and control, loading and unloading, and pollution.

Section III – Physical Damage Coverage
Physical damage coverage is available also as a separate form called the **Business Auto Physical Damage Form**. It covers physical damage only.

Under a Business Auto Policy the insured may select these physical damage coverage options:
1) Comprehensive
2) Collision and
3) Specific Perils Coverage - an alternate to comprehensive coverage.

Physical Damage Exclusions include war, nuclear hazards, racing activities, wear and tear, freezing, mechanical breakdown, and loss to tapes, records, discs, radar devices, and related accessories.

Section IV – Business Auto Conditions includes appraisal, insured's duties in the case of loss, legal actions, transfer of rights and subrogation.

Section V – Definitions define terms such as: accident, auto, mobile equipment, and trailers.

Split Limits provide different amounts of coverage for bodily injury and property damage.

Combined Single Limit combines bodily injury and property damage into one single limit of protection.

Auto medical payments are non-liability coverage for medical expenses if the insured or passengers' health care insurance does not cover the costs.

Who is an insured?
The following are "insureds":
a. You for any covered "auto".
b. Anyone else while using with your permission a covered "auto" you own, hire or borrow.
c. Anyone liable for the conduct of an "insured" described above but only to the extent of that liability.

Types of Autos
Autos may be Owned, Non-owned, Hired, Temporary Substitute or Newly Acquired Autos.

Transportation Expense and Rental Reimbursement Expense If the car is stolen, it pays $20 per day after a 48 hour waiting period to a maximum of $600. If the car is damaged, the waiting period is 24 hours.

1. The Business Auto Coverage Form would be used to insure the commercial auto risks of

A. Garages
B. Truckers
C. Retail stores
D. Motor carriers

2. Business auto physical damage covers

A. Earthquake
B. Wear and tear
C. Nuclear hazards
D. Mechanical breakdown

3. Business Auto Liability coverage includes

A. Intentional acts
B. Workers compensation exposures
C. Costs to defend, investigate and settle all suits
D. Damage to property transported and in the care, custody and control of the insured

4. The type of insurance designed to pay the insured for bodily injuries caused by a motorist with no insurance who is at fault is

A. Stacked limits
B. Uninsured motorist
C. Underinsured motorist
D. Excess over insurance

5. Which of the following is NOT an available business auto physical damage coverage agreement?

A. Special perils
B. Specific perils
C. Collision coverage
D. Comprehensive coverage

6. Physical damage coverage under the business auto covers

A. Radar devices
B. Racing activities
C. Mechanical breakdown
D. Rounding a curve and rolling a car

7. When different amounts of coverage are provided for bodily injury and property damage, it is referred to as

A. Split limits
B. Statutory limits
C. Aggregate limits
D. Combined single limits

8. Under an Auto Policy, how much would be paid under transportation expense for a stolen auto after 5 days?

A. $40
B. $60
C. $80
D. $100

1-C   2-A   3-C   4-B   5-A   6-D   7-A   8-B

GARAGE COVERAGE FORM

Section I – Covered Autos Coverage applies to the autos identified in the declarations.

Section II - Garage Liability includes the coverage of the owners, landlords and tenants (O. L. & T.) plus products and completed operations (products sold or work performed) plus auto liability plus premises and operations.

It excludes care, custody and control and eliminates coverage for damage to autos belonging to customers which are in the care of the insured.

Section III - Garagekeepers covers damage to customers vehicles in the insured's care, custody and control.

Individual Insured and Drive Other Car (DOC)

Individual named insured endorsement. Vehicles listed on a commercial auto insurance policy having the Individual Named Insured Endorsement are covered for personal or non-business use by individuals or sole proprietors. The endorsement also covers a resident spouse or relatives if they are driving a non-owned vehicle.

Drive other car coverage can provide protection for the executive of a Partnership or Corporation or their spouse when driving a non-owned vehicle, such as a vehicle that is rented or borrowed.

1. Garage liability coverage includes

A. Product recall
B. Failure to complete repairs as promised
C. Premises operations and completed operations
D. Property damage to the garages' defective products

2. Garagekeepers coverage under the garage coverage form covers

A. Product liability
B. Premises operations
C. Bodily injury and property damage due to liquor liability
D. Damage to a customer's auto while the insured is servicing the vehicle

3. Garagekeepers insurance does NOT cover the insured's liability for damage for

A. Storing a customers auto
B. Repairing a customers auto
C. Servicing a customers auto
D. Dealers auto inventory held for sale

4. The endorsement needed by an executive who is furnished a company auto, but does not own or carry personal auto insurance is the

A. Employees as Insureds
B. Drive other Car Coverage
C. Individual Named Insureds
D. Deductible Liability Coverage

1-C   2-D   3-D   4-B

III. COMMERCIAL GENERAL LIABILITY

Exposures
Business firms have liability exposure in 6 areas.

Premises and operations provides coverage at the insured's business location for
1) ownership and maintenance of premises and
2) conduct of business operations.

Products and completed operations provides coverage for exposures away from the insured's business location for
3) products (negligence and warranty) and
4) completed operations.

Other:
5) contingent liability
6) contractual liability

Commercial general liability coverage forms

(Coverage A) Bodily injury and property damage liability Property damage includes physical damage to, destruction of, and loss of use of damaged tangible property during the policy period.

Exclusions A through N include expected or intended injury, contractual assumptions (except for lease of premises agreement, sidetrack agreement and elevator maintenance agreement), liquor liability, workers compensation, employer's liability, pollution, aircraft, autos, and watercraft, mobile equipment are excluded while being transported by an auto (it is covered under the Business Auto Policy while it is being towed by an insured auto), war, care, custody and control, damage to the insured's product, damage to the insured's work, property damage to impaired property, and product recall.

Coverage A does cover Fire Legal Liability, Host Liquor Liability, and Contractual Liability.

Occurrence versus claims-made deals with the problem of latent injury, in which the person who suffers the injury may not discover the injury until long after it occurs.

Occurrence
1. Covers injuries and damage which occurred during the policy period, regardless of when a claim was made or suit was brought.

2. Covers claims made at any time for injuries that occur during the policy period.

3. "Occurrence" may be accidental, unexpected, continuous or repeated exposure to conditions over a period of time. It does not have to be sudden.

4. The exact time of the accident need not be readily identifiable.

Claims-made
1. Coverage applies not on the basis of the time at which the injury or damage occurs, but based on the time that the claim is filed with the insurer. Coverage applies only if a claim for damage is first made against any insured during the policy period.

The trigger for coverage is based on the date the claim is first made in writing against an insured for injury or damage that occurred after the policy's retroactive date.

The three **extended reporting periods** include:

Basic 60 day the claim-reporting period of a claims-made policy is extended for 60 days after the expiration of the policy.

Basic 5 year notice of an occurrence to the insured or the insurer during the policy period (or within 60 days of the end of the policy period) triggers an automatic 5-year extended reporting period.

Supplemental is an unlimited extension of the reporting period provided by endorsement and payment of an additional premium. The endorsement cannot be canceled and there is no time limit within which claims must be reported.

The insured must request the supplemental coverage within 60 days after the end of the policy period. It can be activated when the policy is canceled or not renewed, by either the insured or insurer.

1. If a customer falls down and gets hurt on the insured's business location, liability coverage would be provided under

A. Premises liability
B. Contingent liability
C. Contractual liability
D. Completed operations

2. If an insured is held liable for the actions of a subcontractor, this is an example of

A. Product liability
B. Premises liability
C. Contingent liability
D. Contractual liability

3. The Commercial General Liability coverage form includes

A. Loss of use of damaged property
B. Damage to the insured's product
C. Expected or intentional bodily injury
D. Property damage to impaired property

4. The Commercial General Liability coverage form excludes

A. Fire legal liability
B. Host liquor liability
C. Contractual liability
D. Employer's liability

5. When the commercial general liability coverage part covers injuries and damage which occurred during the policy period, regardless of when a claim was made or a suit was brought, it is written on

A. A retroactive basis
B. An occurrence basis
C. A claims-made basis
D. An extended reporting period basis

6. Coverage under the occurrence form of liability is triggered by

A. Injury that occurs after the policy period
B. Only injuries that are reported during the policy period
C. Only injuries that occur and are reported during the policy period
D. Injury that occurs during the policy period, regardless of when it is reported

7. Coverage applies only if a claim for damage is first made against any insured during the policy period on

A. A retroactive basis
B. An occurrence basis
C. A claims-made basis
D. An extended reporting period basis

8. The supplemental extended reporting period of the claims made form is

A. A 5 year extension
B. A 60 day extension
C. A premium free extension
D. An unlimited extension

9. The Supplemental Extended Reporting Period

A. Extends the reporting period for 5 years
B. Cannot be purchased when a business is ceasing operations
C. Applies to claims which occurred and were reported during the policy period
D. Must be requested by the named insured in writing prior to policy termination

10. The insured must request the supplemental coverage within how many days after the end of the policy period?

A. 30 days
B. 60 days
C. 90 days
D. 120 days

1-A   2-C   3-A   4-D   5-B   6-D   7-C   8-D   9-C   10-C

(Coverage B) Personal and advertising injury liability Personal Injury is defined to include: false arrest, detention, or imprisonment, malicious prosecution, wrongful entry into or eviction of a person from a room, dwelling, or premises that the person occupies, or written publication of material that slanders or libels a person, and oral or written publication of material that violates a person's right of privacy.

The triggers of coverage for Personal Injury and Advertising Injury Coverage (and Medical Expenses) are on an occurrence basis under both the claims-made and occurrence versions of the policy.

Personal and Advertising Injury Liability has a sublimit for any one person.

(Coverage C) Medical payments pays reasonable medical expenses incurred within one year of an accident to injured persons, regardless of liability.

Supplementary payments includes up to $250 for the cost of bail bonds, and all reasonable expenses incurred by the insured at the company's request, including loss of earnings up to $250 per day because of time lost from work.

Who is an insured? sole proprietors, partnerships, corporations, and the insured's employees while working within the scope of their employment.

Limits of liability are specific limits that will be paid under the policy.

Damage to Property of Others may be subject to an occurrence and annual aggregate limit.

Owners and contractors protective liability coverage form protects an owner, operator or contractor against loss caused by the negligence of a hired contractor or subcontractor.

Insured contracts include lease or easement agreements, elevator maintenance agreements, sidetrack agreements and contracts required by ordinance.

Pollution liability is excluded but can be added back by these forms:

Pollution liability coverage form provides coverage for bodily injury or property damage caused by a pollution incident including cleanup costs.

Pollution liability limited coverage form also covers bodily injury or property damage but only applies to on-site pollution incidents and does not cover cleanup costs.

Pollution liability coverage extension Endorsement to the CGL adds coverage for bodily injury and property damage but does not remove the exclusion for cleanup costs.

71

1. Personal injury liability

A. Covers malicious prosecution
B. Has no sublimit for any one person
C. Includes physical damage to tangible property
D. Includes incomplete comparisons of competitor's products

2. Medical payments under the CGL cover injuries

A. Related to war
B. To any insured
C. Payable under workers compensation
D. Incurred and reported to the insurer within one year of the date of the accident

3. Coverage C – Medical Payments of the Commercial General Liability excludes

A. Injuries arising from the insured's operations
B. Injuries that occur on premises the insured owns or rents
C. Injuries that occur to a person taking part in athletics
D. Injuries on ways next to premises the insured owns or rents

4. Supplementary payments under the commercial general liability exclude

A. Bail bonds up to $250
B. Tax penalties and interest
C. Loss of earnings up to $250 per day
D. Unlimited legal defense costs which are paid in addition to the policy limit of liability

5. The liability coverage that protects an owner, operator or contractor against loss caused by the negligence of a hired contractor or subcontractor is

A. Contractual liability
B. Premises and operations
C. Products and completed operations
D. Owners and contractors protective liability

6. The Pollution Liability – Limited Form does NOT cover

A. Cleanup costs
B. On a claims made basis
C. Emissions of pollutants into or on land
D. Emissions of pollutants into the atmosphere or water

1-A   2-D   3-C   4-B   5-D   6-A

72

IV. CRIME

Employee Dishonesty covers losses resulting from employee dishonesty and covers money, securities, and other property.

Theft includes any illegal taking of the property of others without their consent. Theft includes both:

Robbery "the taking of property from the care and custody of a person by one who has (a) caused or threatened bodily harm to that person or, (b) committed an obviously unlawful act witnessed by that person."

EXAMPLES: Threat of violence upon a messenger, kidnapping a custodian to gain entry into the premises and theft in the presence of an employee.

Burglary "the taking of property from inside the premises by a person unlawfully entering or leaving the premises as evidenced by marks (visible signs) of forcible entry or exit." EXAMPLE: Forcible entry into locked premises after business hours.

Forgery and Alteration covers the insured worldwide for loss of money resulting from forgery and alteration of outgoing checks, drafts, or promissory notes.

The definition of MONEY includes currency, coins, bank notes, travelers checks, registered checks and money orders held for sale, but not evidence of debt. Evidence of debt is a type of security.

Under the Commercial crime coverage part of the CPP, there is a governmental action exclusion.

V. OTHER TYPES OF CASUALTY POLICIES

BONDS

Bond underwriting is based on character, capacity, and capital. The limit of liability of a bond is called its penalty.

Surety Bonds guarantee obligations through a three-party contract.

1. Principal. The one who owes an obligation to perform or to refrain from doing certain acts.

2. Surety. The one who guarantees the Principal will perform the obligation or refrain from doing the acts. In the event of a loss the surety has the right to collect from the principal any amounts it has been required to pay the obligee.

3. Obligee. The one to whom the Principal and the Surety owe the obligation.

Fidelity Bonds protect employers from any loss of money or property incurred as a result of hiring high-risk job seekers who might engage in employee theft, larceny, or embezzlement.

Judicial bonds "court bonds" are used in the legal process, e.g., bail bonds, appeal bonds, attachment bonds, injunction bonds and fiduciary bonds.

73

1. The crime form covers

A. Computer fraud
B. Theft committed by an insured
C. Indirect or consequential losses
D. Seizure of property by government authority

2. Employee theft coverage

A. Proof of loss may be based on inventory shortage
B. Covers loss resulting from trading in a genuine or fictitious account
C. Covers loss resulting from dishonest use of warehouse receipts
D. Pays for theft committed by an employee either acting alone or in collusion with others

3. The taking of property from the care and custody of a person by the threat of bodily harm is

A. Theft
B. Burglary
C. Robbery
D. Extortion

4. The taking of property from within the premises by unlawful entering as evidenced by marks of forcible entry or exit is

A. Theft
B. Burglary
C. Extortion
D. Robbery

5. The definition of money does NOT include

A. Currency
B. Money orders
C. Evidence of debt
D. Registered checks

6. The commercial crime coverage part of the commercial package policy covers

A. Government seizure
B. Acts committed by third parties
C. Legal expenses relating to a crime loss
D. Loss resulting from a partner's involvement

7. Bond underwriting is based on all of the following EXCEPT

A. Capital
B. Capacity
C. Character
D. Capability

8. The equivalent of an insurance company under a surety bond is the

A. Surety
B. Obligor
C. Obligee
D. Principal

9. A license or permit bond would be appropriate for all of the following EXCEPT

A. Funeral director
B. Private detective
C. Estate administrator
D. Sale of liquor, tobacco, or gasoline

10. The type of judicial bond which guarantees a defendant will appear as required by the court is

A. Bail bond
B. Appeal bond
C. Fiduciary bond
D. Injunction bond

1-A   2-D   3-C   4-B   5-C   6-B   7-D   8-A   9-C   10-A

PROFESSIONAL LIABILITY

Errors and Omissions
E&O professional liability coverage protects the insured against liability for committing an error or omission in the performance of professional duties in the service for clients.

E&O is written for non-medical professions such as accountants, insurance agents, architects, and bankers.

Medical malpractice is written for medical professions such as doctors, physicians, morticians and beauty parlor operators.

Directors and Officers liability protects corporate officers and directors from suits by stockholders or by persons outside the firm alleging mismanagement.

Employment Practices Liability (EPLI) is written for employers who might face litigation alleging discrimination, sexual harassment, retaliation, and other torts. A tort is a wrongdoing that results in injury to another person or damage to property.

UMBRELLA/EXCESS LIABILITY

The coverage of the Personal Umbrella Policy is **broader in scope of coverage** since it covers some liability losses excluded by the personal auto policy and the homeowners policy.

The Commercial Umbrella Policy limits range upward from $1,000,000.

An Umbrella Policy serves 3 functions:
1) excess insurance over other insurance,

2) more comprehensive coverage (certain losses excluded by primary insurance are covered), and

3) drop down coverage after the underlying insurance is exhausted.

Umbrella Liability Policies provide coverage for the basic exposures of Bodily Injury, Property Damage, Personal Injury, and Advertising Liability. Defective products liability is NOT usually covered under an umbrella policy.

It is written only for insureds that have a broad and substantial program of underlying coverage.

Each insurer draws up its own contract as there is no "standard" form of umbrella liability policy. All policies include a pollution liability exclusion.

When the umbrella covers a loss that is excluded by the underlying policies, the insured choses a retention limit from $250 to $10,000 which acts like a deductible. This self-insured deductible would not apply to losses covered by the underlying liability coverage.

In addition, the umbrella can function as **excess liability** by covering those losses in excess of the underlying insurance policy limits.

1. Errors and Omissions insurance would most likely be carried by

A. Dentists
B. Surgeons
C. Beauticians
D. Insurance agents

2. Errors and Omissions insurance would NOT be carried by

A. Doctors
B. Engineers
C. Architects
D. Financial advisors

3. Directors and officers liability would cover legal action brought against directors for all of the following EXCEPT

A. Employment practices
B. Alleged mismanagement
C. Failing to act in the corporation's best interest
D. Suits by creditors or competitors from outside the corporation

4. Employment practices liability excludes

A. Work related sexual harassment
B. Serving alcohol in the workplace
C. Refusal to employ a person based on discrimination
D. Work related verbal or emotional abuse directed a person relating to national origin

5. The Personal Umbrella Policy would NOT function as excess insurance over

A. Section II of the Homeowners Policy
B. Personal automobile liability coverage
C. Personal automobile collision coverage
D. Comprehensive personal liability coverage

6. When an insured fails to maintain the underlying liability limits as required by the Personal Umbrella Policy

A. All coverages would be voided
B. It would have no effect on the umbrella coverage
C. The insurer would have to pay the self-insured retention limit
D. The insured would be responsible for the difference between the required amount and the umbrella's threshold

7. The amount of a loss the insured must cover out of pocket under a personal umbrella for those losses that are excluded by the underlying policy is called a

A. Policy limit
B. Elimination limit
C. Retroactive limit
D. Self-insured retention limit

8. The commercial umbrella does NOT cover

A. Usual or everyday exposures of business risk
B. A self-insured retention of usually a minimum of $10,000
C. Coverage where the underlying coverage does not respond
D. Excess coverage over the required underlying liability limits of the primary policy

1-D   2-A   3-A   4-B   5-C   6-D   7-D   8-A

VI. IOWA LAWS, RULES, AND REGULATIONS PERTINENT TO CASUALTY INSURANCE ONLY

A. Iowa Auto Insurance Plan (Assigned Risk)

Insured told of alternate coverage. When automobile bodily injury and property damage liability coverage is canceled or not renewed, other than for nonpayment of premium, the insurer shall notify the named insured of the insured's possible eligibility for automobile liability insurance through the Iowa automobile insurance plan. Such notice shall accompany the notice of cancellation or intent not to renew.

B. Private-passenger automobile insurance

1. Uninsured/Underinsured motorists coverage

UM/UIM rejection Uninsured motorist coverage must be included in all automobile policies issued in Iowa unless specifically rejected by the insured.

In Iowa the insurer has no subrogation right with respect to payments made under Uninsured Motorist Coverage for bodily injury.

Required limits Coverage is required to be provided in amounts of $20,000/$40,000 for bodily injury or death.

Notice regarding coverage
"Uninsured/Underinsured coverage does not cover damage to your vehicle. It provides benefits only for bodily injury caused by an uninsured or underinsured motorist. If you wish to be insured for damage done to your vehicle, you must have collision coverage. Please check your policy to make sure you have the coverage desired."

77

1. When an auto policy is cancelled or nonrenewed, other than for nonpayment of premium, the insurer shall notify the named insured of the possible eligibility for auto coverage through the

A. NAIC
B. FAIR Plan
C. Iowa Automobile Insurance Plan
D. Iowa Insurance Guaranty Association

2. Uninsured motorist coverage

A. Is not available in Iowa
B. Is issued only for higher amounts of insurance
C. Must be included in all automobile policies issued in Iowa
D. Must be included in all automobile policies issued in Iowa unless specifically rejected by the insured

3. In Iowa, with respect to payments made under Uninsured Motorist Coverage for bodily injury, the insurer has

A. A duty to subrogate
B. No subrogation rights
C. Limited subrogation rights
D. A duty to make payment without limit

4. The minimum required limits for Uninsured/Underinsured motorist coverage are

A. $15,000/$30,000
B. $20,000/$40,000
C. $30,000/$55,000
D. $50,000/$1000,000

5. Uninsured/Underinsured coverage provides benefits only for

A. Bodily injury
B. Personal injury
C. Property damage
D. Bodily injury and property damage

1-C   2-D   3-B   4-B   5-A

2. Proof of financial responsibility
Iowa Motor Vehicle Financial Responsibility Law
All owners of a motor vehicle must show financial responsibility if a vehicle is stopped by a law officer or at the time of an accident that results in bodily injury or property damage in excess of $1,000.

Individuals must carry in the vehicle an insurance identification card as evidence of financial responsibility.

Proof of financial responsibility.
It requires a driver to show proof of financial responsibility in the amount of $20,000/$40,000/$15,000.

$20,000 is the minimum requirement of liability paid to a single individual for bodily injury ($20,000 per person), $40,000 per occurrence for bodily injury, and $15,000 per occurrence for property damage.

Policies written with a single limit of liability for BI and property damage must be written with a single limit of $55,000.

3. Cancellation and nonrenewal.
Grounds. Cancellation is permitted only for nonpayment of premium; nonpayment of dues; fraud or material misrepresentation; violation of the terms or conditions of the policy; and suspension or revocation of the driver's license.

Notice. Notice is required at least 10 days prior if the policy has been in effect for less than 60 days.

For policies in effect for more than 60 days, at least 10 days for nonpayment of premium and 20 days for other grounds.

Notice of eligibility in assigned risk plan
All cancellation notices must notify the insured of the eligibility of coverage through the Assigned Risk Plan.

Nonrenewal is permitted with 30 days advance notice.

4. Aftermarket parts regulation

Guidelines for use of aftermarket crash parts in motor vehicles.

Like kind and quality. An insurer shall not require the use of aftermarket crash parts in the repair of an automobile unless the aftermarket crash part is certified by a nationally recognized entity to be at least equal in kind and quality to the original equipment manufacturer part in terms of fit, quality and performance, or that the part complies with federal safety standards.

Contents of notice. Any automobile insurance policy delivered in this state that pays benefits based on the cost of aftermarket crash parts or that requires the insured to pay the difference between the cost of original equipment manufacturer parts and the cost of aftermarket crash parts shall include a notice which contains and is limited to the following language:

NOTICE—PAYMENT FOR AFTERMARKET CRASH PARTS Physical damage coverage under this policy includes payment for aftermarket crash parts. If you repair the vehicle using more expensive original equipment manufacturer (OEM) parts, you may pay the difference. Any warranties applicable to these replacement parts are provided by the manufacturer or distributor of these parts rather than the manufacturer of your vehicle.

This notice is required with all newly issued policies no later than at the time of delivery of the policy.

It may be a separate form or stamped on the declaration page of the policy.

1. All of the following are required under the Iowa Motor Vehicle Financial Responsibility Law EXCEPT

A. Financial liability coverage is in effect for the motor vehicle
B. Financial liability coverage is required to renew a driver's license
C. The driver has in the motor vehicle a financial liability card issued for the vehicle
D. A peace officer may require exhibition of the proof of insurance card issued for the vehicle

2. The required limits of liability to meet the financial responsibility requirements under the Iowa Motor Vehicle Responsibility Law are

A. 15/30/15
B. 20/30/15
C. 20/40/15
D. 20/45/20

3. The required minimum of property damage liability under the Iowa Motor Vehicle Financial Responsibility Law is

A. $10,000
B. $15,000
C. $20,000
D. $40,000

4. Policies written with a single limit of liability for BI and property damage must be written with a single limit of

A. $20,000
B. $40,000
C. $55,000
D. $75,000

5. Advance notice for nonpayment of premium must be given at least

A. 10 days
B. 15 days
C. 20 days
D. 30 days

6. An auto policy may NOT be cancelled because of

A. Nonpayment of premium
B. Occupation of the insured
C. Fraud or material misrepresentation
D. Violation of the terms or conditions of the policy

7. Notice of cancellation of a policy is not effective unless it is based on the insured's

A. Age
B. Occupation
C. Place of residence
D. Drivers license being suspended

8. Advance Notice of Nonrenewal must be how many days prior to the policy's expiration?

A. 15 days
B. 20 days
C. 30 days
D. 45 days

9. Aftermarket parts regulations does NOT state that

A. The estimate must clearly identify each part proposed to be used which is an aftermarket part
B. An aftermarket crash part must have affixed or inscribed the logo or name of its manufacturer
C. A repair facility may use aftermarket crash parts without disclosing the proposed use of such parts
D. A repair facility installing an aftermarket crash part must install the part so that the manufacturer's logo or name is visible upon inspection

10. All of the following are true under the "Notice-payment for aftermarket crash parts" EXCEPT

A. The insured pays the difference between the original equipment manufacturer parts and the aftermarket crash parts
B. The notice is required with all newly issued policies
C. The notice may be a separate form or stamped on the declaration page of the policy
D. The vehicle manufacturer provides any warranties applicable to aftermarket crash parts

1-B   2-C   3-B   4-C   5-A   6-B   7-D   8-C   9-C   10-D

C. Workers compensation

1. Definitions
The following persons shall not be deemed "workers" or "employees":

a. A person whose employment is purely casual and not for the purpose of the employer's trade or business.

b. An independent contractor

c. An owner-operator of a truck

d. Directors of a corporation who are not at the same time employees of the corporation

e. Proprietors, limited liability company members, and partners who have not elected to be covered by the workers' compensation law.

2. Covered employment
Workers compensation does NOT apply to:

1. Casual employees and domestic employees who earn less than $1,500 during the twelve consecutive months prior to the injury.

2. Persons engaged in agriculture employed by an employer whose total cash payroll to one or more persons amounted to less than $2,500 during the preceding calendar year.

Proprietors, limited liability company members, and partners
A proprietor, limited liability company member, or partner who is actively engaged in the proprietor's, limited liability company member's, or partner's business on a substantially full-time basis, may elect to be covered by the workers' compensation law of this state by purchasing valid workers' compensation insurance specifically including the proprietor, limited liability company member, or partner.

Compulsory
Where the state, county, municipal corporation, school corporation, area education agency, or city under any form of government is the employer, these provisions shall be exclusive, compulsory, and obligatory upon both employer and employee. Elected and appointed officials shall be employees.

Acceptance presumed--notice to nonresident employers
1. Every employer shall provide, secure, and pay compensation for any and all personal injuries sustained by an employee arising out of and in the course of the employment, and in such cases, the employer shall be relieved from other liability for recovery of damages or other compensation for such personal injury.

2. Any nonresident employer for whom services are performed within this state by any employee, is deemed to be doing business in this state and shall be subject to the jurisdiction of the workers' compensation commissioner and to all of the provisions as to any and all personal injuries sustained by the employee arising out of and in the course of such employment within this state.

Willful injury—intoxication
No compensation under this chapter shall be allowed for an injury caused:

1. By the employee's willful intent to injure the employee's self or to willfully injure another.

2. By the employee's intoxication, which did not arise out of and in the course of employment but which was due to the effects of alcohol or another narcotic, depressant, stimulant, hallucinogenic, or hypnotic drug not prescribed by an authorized medical practitioner, if the intoxication was a substantial factor in causing the injury.

3. By the willful act of a third party directed against the employee for reasons personal to such employee.

Rights of employee exclusive
The rights and remedies shall be the exclusive and only rights and remedies of the employee against the employer or against any other employee.

1. Under the Iowa workers compensation laws, which of the following is not an employee?

A. School teachers
B. Municipal workers
C. Appointed officials
D. An independent contractor

2. An example of a person exempt from workers compensation is

A. A bus driver
B. An owner-operator of a truck
C. A conservation officer at a state park
D. A director of a corporation who is an employee of the corporation

3. The workers compensation laws of Iowa do NOT apply to

A. Partners
B. Aviation
C. Meat packers
D. Part time employees

4. Workers compensation laws cover

A. Independent contractors
B. Employees injured by fellow employees
C. Domestic and casual employees who earn less than $1,500 from the employer during the 12 consecutive months prior to an injury
D. Persons employed in agriculture by an employer whose total cash payments to all such employees is less than $2,500 a year or who does not employ one such person regularly

5. Persons engaged in agriculture employed by an employer whose total cash payroll to one or more persons amounted to less than how much during the preceding calendar year.

A. $600
B. $1,500
C. $2,500
D. $5,000

6. An employer shall provide compensation for personal injuries arising out of

A. The employee's employment
B. The employee's intoxication
C. Employment and personal activities
D. The employee's willful intent to injure another

7. A compensable occupational disease under workers compensation MUST

A. Have been foreseen or expected
B. Be independent of the employment
C. Follow from a hazard outside of the occupation
D. Have a direct causal connection with the employment

8. Nonresident employers who perform services within the state of Iowa

A. Are subject to Iowa workers compensation law
B. Can "opt-out" of Iowa workers compensation law
C. Are exempt from Iowa workers compensation law
D. Can "opt-in" and be subject to Iowa workers compensation law

9. Employees cannot sue their employers in court to obtain additional compensation for work related injuries because workers compensation insurance is always

A. Elective
B. Compulsory
C. Competitive
D. An exclusive remedy

10. Workers compensation covers

A. Work related diseases
B. Employees intoxication
C. Employee's willful intent to injure himself, herself or another person
D. Willful act of a third party directed against the employee for personal reasons

1-D   2-B   3-A   4-D   5-C   6-A   7-D   8-A   9-D   10-A

Notice of injury--failure to give
No compensation shall be allowed unless the employer or the employer's representative shall have actual knowledge of the occurrence of an injury received within **90 days** from the date of the occurrence of the injury.

3. Benefits provided

Services
The employer shall furnish reasonable surgical, medical, dental, osteopathic, chiropractic, podiatric, physical rehabilitation, nursing, ambulance and hospital services and supplies and shall allow reasonably necessary transportation expenses incurred for such services. The employer shall also furnish reasonable and necessary crutches, artificial members and appliances but shall not be required to furnish more than one set of permanent prosthetic devices.

Burial expense
When death ensues from the injury, the employer shall pay the reasonable expenses of burial of such employee, not **to exceed $7,500**.

When compensation begins
Except as to injuries resulting in permanent partial disability, compensation shall begin on the **fourth day** of disability after the injury.

If the period of incapacity extends beyond the fourteenth day following the date of injury, then the compensation due during the third week shall be increased by adding thereto an amount equal to three days of compensation.

4. Covered injuries

Note: The **Second Injury Fund** helps pay compensation for individuals who were previously injured. The second injury fund promotes the hiring of disabled workers and removes the financial penalty on the employer who hires an individual with a greater probability of future injury and higher claims frequency.

Temporary disabilities

Temporary total disability weekly compensation benefits are paid by the employer until the employee has returned to work or is medically capable of returning to employment substantially similar to the employment in which the employee was engaged at the time of injury, whichever occurs first.

Temporary partial disability" or "temporarily, partially disabled" means the condition of an employee for whom it is medically indicated that the employee is not capable of returning to employment substantially similar to the employment in which the employee was engaged at the time of injury, but is able to perform other work consistent with the employee's disability.

The **temporary partial benefit** shall be **sixty-six and two-thirds percent** of the difference between the employee's weekly earnings at the time of injury and the employee's actual gross weekly income from employment during the period of temporary partial disability.

83

1. Under workers compensation, employees or their representatives must notify their employer of injury within

A. 30 days
B. 60 days
C. 90 days
D. 120 days

2. Workers compensation would NOT provide benefits for

A. Death benefits
B. General damages
C. Rehabilitation benefits
D. Unlimited medical benefits

3. Workers Compensation pays for burial expense not to exceed

A. $5,000
B. $7,500
C. $10,000
D. $12,500

4. Workers compensation payments generally begin how many days after the injury?

A. 1 day
B. 2 days
C. 3 days
D. 4 days

5. The hiring of individuals who were previously injured is promoted by the

A. Iowa Assigned Risk Fund
B. Iowa Second Injury Fund
C. Iowa Civil Rights Commission
D. Iowa Association of Insurance and Financial Advisors

6. The second injury fund does NOT

A. Provide funds to employees with more than one injury
B. Encourage employers to hire workers with pre-existing disabilities
C. Pay some or all of the additional compensation because of a second injury
D. Lessen the financial burden of hiring workers who were previously injured

7. The type of disability in which the employee is medically capable of returning to employment substantially similar to the employment in which the employee was engaged at the time of injury is

A. Temporary total
B. Permanent total
C. Permanent partial
D. Temporary partial

8. The type of disability in which the employee is not capable of returning to employment substantially similar to the employment in which the employee was engaged at the time of injury, but is able to perform other work consistent with the employee's disability is

A. Temporary total
B. Permanent total
C. Permanent partial
D. Temporary partial

9. The temporary partial benefit is what percent?

A. 33%
B. 50%
C. 66 2/3 %
D. 80%

1-C   2-B   3-B   4-D   5-B   6-A   7-A   8-D   9-C

Permanent disabilities

An employee shall receive compensation for permanent disabilities. In addition, payment is made during the healing period for permanent partial disabilities.

Healing period If an employee has suffered a personal injury causing permanent partial disability, the employer shall pay to the employee compensation for a healing period, beginning on the first day of disability after the injury.

Permanent partial disabilities Compensation for permanent partial disability shall begin at the termination of the healing period.

The compensation shall be based upon the extent of the disability and upon the basis of **eighty percent per week of the employee's average spendable weekly earnings**.

A schedule lists various cases of permanent partial disability and the compensation paid for each, ranging from the loss of a thumb (sixty weeks) up to the loss of both arms, or both hands, or both feet, or both legs, or both eyes, or any two thereof (five hundred weeks).

Permanent total disability Compensation for an injury causing permanent total disability shall be upon the basis of **eighty percent** per week of the employee's average spendable weekly earnings.

Occupational Disease

Occupational disease defined
Occupational diseases shall be only those diseases which arise out of and in the course of the employee's employment.

Compensation payable
All employees who shall become disabled from an occupational disease shall receive compensation, reasonable surgical, medical, osteopathic, chiropractic, physical rehabilitation, nursing and hospital services and supplies, and burial expenses.

1. Healing period disability benefits begin on the

A. First day of disability
B. Fourth day of disability
C. Tenth day of disability
D. Fifteenth day of disability

2. The permanent partial and permanent total disability benefit is what percent?

A. 33%
B. 50%
C. 66 2/3 %
D. 80%

3. Which type of disability benefit has a schedule of compensation based on the loss?

A. Temporary total
B. Permanent total
C. Permanent partial
D. Temporary partial

4. Workers compensation insurance would NOT pay for a disease which

A. Arises out of and in the course of the employee's employment
B. Followed as a natural incident from injurious exposure occasioned by the nature of the employment
C. Had its origin in a risk connected with the employment
D. Follows from a hazard to which an employee has been equally exposed outside of their occupation

1-A   2-D   3-C   4-D

STUDY TIPS

Common Sense Tips for Exam Preparation

I am often asked, "What is the best way to study for the test?" Over the years, I have found the following tips helpful in passing an exam.

First of all, get a handle on the Scope of the test. There is absolutely no need to study things that are outside the parameters of the exam when you are beginning.

In this regard, the Insurance Licensing Candidate Handbook contains an outline of the current exam content. It is available from Pearson VUE at **www.pearsonvue.com**

Next, keep your studying Focused. When you focus on the specific topics on the exam outline, then you are able to make sure you are covering all the necessary topics.

Focusing on the major points associated with each outline topic will keep you from chasing down rabbit trails that are not on the exam. Do not stray away from the actual exam material.

Get a study buddy to help prepare. This can be someone at work who is currently studying or who has already passed the exam. Quiz each other. Try to stump the other person.

You can even hand the material to a family member who is not in the business and say, "Here, quiz me!"

It seems that children especially take delight in trying to stump their parents. On the other hand they can also be very encouraging.

When you make a game of it, studying is much less stressful and more enjoyable.

By all accounts, it helps to take a crash course from a reputable training center. In my seminar, we systematically go through the exam outline topic-by-topic. We learn those testing points that we know will be on the exam.

You will benefit by having the information presented to you in a formal manner where your focus is solely on the exam content.

In the classroom, there are no distractions, no family to attend to, and no employer interrupting your study time. You have the entire day to focus on one thing: learning enough to pass your exam the first time.

You are learning from someone who knows the material, knows the exam, and is an open book for any questions you may have. My classroom seminar schedule and registration is on my website at **www.IowaInsuranceSeminar.com**

The need for advance preparation seems to vary among students. Some students could read all the manuals ever written before coming to class and still not feel prepared. Others just register for the crash course. They use only the classroom materials and do just fine. Of course, many folks use only this study manual and are successful.

Reading the actual policies on which you will be tested is of great benefit if you have access to the current version as stated on the study outline. Although they are legal contracts written by lawyers, they contain many of the phrases and terms used by the exam writers.

As the exam has become more difficult, the trend has been toward more students reading something before class to get over the initial hurdle of insurance terms and policy components.

It is easiest to read a study manual in bits-and-pieces rather than try to conquer a whole chapter or manual in a single marathon. Carry this manual with you and sneak-a-peek when you have those odd spare moments.

TESTING TIPS

Now let's talk about some tips for the exam itself.

First of all, review your fact sheet of difficult points to remember just before you go into the exam. Then write out a listing of these hard to remember testing points when you sit down at the computer and before you begin the exam.

Since the clock doesn't start until you actually click the exam start button, the time spent writing out your crib sheet will not count against you.

The testing center will provide a sheet of blank scratch paper or an erasable white board to write down your key "things-to-remember".

When taking the exam, you can allocate your time for each question any way you want to.

You can spend 10 seconds or 10 minutes on a question. It doesn't matter.

However, it is best to answer a question and mark it for review if you are uncertain. Do not agonize and fret over it.

Take your best guess and move on. Come back later if you have time.

A good rule of thumb is "Do not change your answer" unless you clearly recognize a need for the change.

Studies show that in the majority of cases students talk themselves out of the correct answer!

In any event, the last answer you mark will be your answer when time runs out or when you terminate the exam.

Another helpful hint is to read the stem of the question at least twice before looking at the possible answers. This helps to clearly understand the question.

If you just skim the question and then jump immediately to the answers, the answers begin to color your understanding of the actual question.

Your mind reads things into the question that are not there and misses important words that are there.

And finally, watch out for key words such as: all, always, only, never, not, and of course the most despised multiple choice word "EXCEPT".

Ideally, you should be well rested and prepared the day of the exam. It is most beneficial to have a good meal the night before and get a good night's sleep. Follow your normal routine if possible.

Naturally in preparing for an exam, procrastination tends to take its' toll.

A late night cram session or pulling an all-nighter does little to help . . . unless you have done no advance study whatsoever!

I believe the best piece of advice is to continue to study right up to the minute you take the exam.

You never know when you may learn that one last testing point that puts you in the pass column and into a successful career.

NOTES

Made in the USA
Monee, IL
29 January 2025

11244678R00052